JERRY FALWELL

CAPTURING
A TOWN
FOR CHRIST

ELMER TOWNS

FLEMING H. REVELL COMPANY
OLD TAPPAN, NEW JERSEY

Scripture quotations in this volume are from the King James Version of
the Bible.

Library of Congress Cataloging in Publication Data

Towns, Elmer L
   Capturing a town for Christ.

   1. Thomas Road Baptist Church. 2. Falwell, Jerry.
3. Evangelistic work—Lynchburg, Va. I. Title.
BX6480.L94T488   286'.1755'671   73-1869
ISBN 0-8007-0598-X
ISBN 0-8007-0606-4 (pbk)

CONTENTS

Foreword by Dr. Jerry Falwell   5

Part One MIRACLES AT THOMAS ROAD   9

1   The Largest Sunday School Since Pentecost   12

2   Putting It All Together   19

3   Thomas Road Baptist Church Is People   49

4   What Is a Great Church?   75

5   Capturing a Town for Christ   86

Part Two MESSAGES OF THOMAS ROAD   109

6   The Church at Antioch   111

7   Becoming a Champion   128

8   Feudin', Fussin', and Frettin'   142

9   The Will of God   152

10   I Can Do All Things But . . .   162

11   The Day of Great Men Has Not Passed   175

12   What Makes a Failure?   184

To
some of the greatest
workers in the world,
all the staff of
Thomas Road Baptist Church

ACKNOWLEDGMENTS

I would like to remember the following for their dedicated work: Robert Creasy, Jeanette and George Hogan, Dusty Rhodes, Rick Rogers, Calvin Combs, Jean Evans, Sam Towns, and George Fay. These are not on the pastoral staff nor are they in the spotlight, but I have appreciated their quiet, efficient work for God. I will probably hurt some feelings by leaving out others I should have mentioned, but these persons come to my mind for faithfulness to their duty.

4

FOREWORD

I have often preached that the greatest church since Pentecost is yet to be built. Why not? We have more tools at hand to build a greater church than any previous generation ever had. The Jerusalem church members saturated their own community and were accused, ". . . ye have filled Jerusalem with your doctrine" (Acts 5:28). This church was so powerful in its outreach that within a few years its critics accused, "These that have turned the world upside down are come hither also" (Acts 17:6). The early church *was* a great church and the members did it without the modern tools that we have at our disposal today. We have more tools than any other generation, therefore we ought to build the greatest church ever. God has given us television, radio, expressways, amplifying systems, high-speed automobiles, school buses, airplanes, and more technical skills and knowledge of our world than any other generation. These tools will not build a great church; a great church is built on the teaching of the Word of God, the power of the Holy Spirit, and transformed lives undergirded with prayer. However, these tools should make it possible to saturate the greater population areas we have in the United States, hence building the greatest church since Pentecost.

Many might argue that we have more sin in our society than ever before, making it impossible to build a great church. The light that shines the brightest, contrasts with the night that it illuminates. Therefore, our churches ought to have a greater impact on our communities and be greater in numbers, involvement, influence, and changed lives.

Dr. Towns has preached in more large churches than any man, having spoken in seventy-three of the one hundred largest churches in America. His books, observations, and annual listing of the one hundred largest Sunday schools qualify him as the outstanding authority on Sunday schools and church growth. His influence on the recent growth at Thomas Road Baptist Church has been invaluable, especially his Twelve Disciple Campaign and lessons that pushed our attendance over six thousand for twelve consecutive weeks during the spring of 1972. We are fortunate to have him as a part of our staff.

As you probably know, I preach from my heart as God leads me, sometimes using notes. I do not preach from a manuscript. The Spirit of God must have freedom to lead the preacher. I must have liberty to emphasize those truths laid upon my heart. I appreciate the editing of the sermons in this book by Dr. Towns from transcribed recordings.

My prayer is that God would bless this book to your heart. Like the Thomas Road Baptist Church, this book exists for the glory of God and the salvation of souls. The sermons, testimonies, and stories are included to communicate the life of Thomas Road to you, the reader. I wish all of you could visit us in Lynchburg, but some of you won't make it, so we are attempting to bring Thomas Road Baptist Church to you. But if you can, come visit us on your vacation or during a holiday. We always have visitors in the service and I want to meet you when you attend my church.

God has given us unparalleled growth in these past two years. Our Sunday-school attendance doubled in that period of time, and our total financial income has jumped twelve times. We now receive in one month what was our annual income two years ago. I sincerely believe the greatest days of Thomas Road Baptist Church are before us. We intend to hire more staff members, build more buildings, purchase more TV time, secure more printing presses, and rent more computers. We will do whatever is possible and necessary to reach the world for Christ. I will expend all my energies to win as many as possible to Christ, so long as God gives me strength. I would like to preach the gospel on every TV station in the free world. That would be carrying out the command of Christ.

I want to build the greatest church since Pentecost, not for personal fame, but for lost souls. We have come through the generation of small and interdenominational missions, only to find ourselves further behind in reaching lost people than we were decades ago. I appreciate what our Christian forefathers did, but I believe the key to evangelism is the local church and every church attempting to reach as many for Christ, in every way possible, at every time possible. This will result in every church growing larger and stronger. I have many close friends who pastor other large superaggressive churches, having gone to school with some of these men at Baptist Bible College, Springfield, Missouri. When I say I want to build the largest church since Pentecost, I am not in competition with them. I compete for God against Satan. My eyes are not on those who run beside me, my eyes are on the goal (Philippians 3:13,14). I want every Bible-preaching church to grow and win souls. We at Thomas Road Baptist Church want our example to motivate other churches to superaggressive evangelism. That is why this book is written.

JERRY FALWELL

Part One

MIRACLES
AT THOMAS ROAD

Many religious organizations claim to have miracles, but very few outside of the loyal members actually believe the claim of miracles. Because so many religious people claim to experience miracles, a definition of the word as used in this book is in order.

The average man on the street identifies a miracle as an act that breaks the laws of nature, such as walking on water or healing an incurable disease. But a strict biblical definition of a miracle is "a transcending of the laws, rather than breaking of the laws of nature." Since God created natural laws, He can go beyond them for His purpose. Hence, a miracle is the work of God, accomplishing His results in an unexpected way.

Thomas Road Baptist Church, like most other religious groups, claims to have the blessing of Almighty God upon its efforts. However, the leadership does not claim to experience the supernatural signs and wonders that accompanied Christ. Those signs were authority for the message which the Lord preached. Jerry Falwell and other workers at Thomas Road Baptist Church preach the same message as Christ, that found in the Word of God. Christ promised that those who followed Him would do even greater works than He did. "Verily, verily, I say unto you, He that believeth on me, the works that I do shall he do also; and greater works than these shall he do; because I go unto my Father" (John 14:12). The greater works than Christ are the changed lives and dynamic, growing churches that result from obedience to Christ. The miracles at Thomas Road Baptist Church are those supernatural results that should accompany the honest preaching of the gospel: drunks are sobered up, broken homes are restored, youth finds identity and purpose in life, former convicts desire to live honest lives, the church grows in size and diversity of ministry, and whole sections of the population are saturated with the gospel.

The first section of this book deals with miracles, where God works unexpectedly in a small southern town reaching the whole world with the gospel. There are unexpected crowds, resulting in phenomenal attendance (Chapter 1). There are unexpected avenues of service whereby the total needs of man become the launching pad to minister to the total population (Chapters 2 and 4). There are unexpected results in the lives of alcoholics, youths, convicts, blue-collar workers, and the elite (Chapter 3). There are unexpected results from the quality ministry resulting in a great church (Chapter 4).

The Thomas Road Baptist Church was begun in June, 1956, when thirty-five adults and their children gathered for the first meeting in the Mountain View Elementary School in Lynchburg, Virginia, a school Jerry Falwell had attended as a boy.

The new church met in the Mountain View School for one Sunday only, then moved to its present site on Thomas Road. At that time a fifty-by-thirty-foot building stood on the property. This building had been a grocery store and later a beverage bottling company. The building was a mess—tall weeds on the grounds, a powdery white dust covering the exterior, and cola syrup over the walls and floor. Members worked every night scrubbing floors and washing walls. A platform was constructed at one end of the empty building and church began.

It is unlikely that any of them, in their fondest dreams, ever contemplated the phenomenal growth and ministry of Thomas Road Baptist Church in the next sixteen years. This has indeed been a twentieth-century miracle.

1

THE LARGEST SUNDAY SCHOOL
SINCE PENTECOST

The largest Sunday school since Pentecost is said to have met at Thomas Road Baptist Church, on June 25, 1972, when 19,020 people assembled on the sixteenth anniversary of the church for the annual Homecoming Service. Since the buildings on Thomas Road were not large enough, the Lynchburg Municipal Stadium was rented. The sixteen-thousand-seat football stadium was adapted for the massive Sunday school. Five thousand folding chairs were set up on the playing field. A gigantic stage was constructed on the north end, with a huge billboard, "The Old-Time Gospel Hour" and the words 16TH ANNIVERSARY, THOMAS ROAD BAPTIST CHURCH. Three hours before Sunday-school time, the crowd began trickling in. Later, when the Sunday-school buses arrived, people poured into the stadium, filling the folding seats on the playing surface and spilling over into the stands. A high-school student, Wayne Mullin, Jr., came from Rochester, New York, just to be present for the largest Sunday school of all time. The Associated Press and *Newsweek* magazine sent reporters; local news photographers were snapping pictures. Editors from Christian magazines observed the crowd and Bob Hill, Managing Editor of *Christian Life* magazine, Wheaton, Illinois, stated, "I had to come and see for myself."

Hurricane Agnes battered Virginia with torrential downpours and record-breaking floods two days before Homecoming. The skeptics asked Jerry Falwell, pastor, what would happen if Homecoming were washed out. Falwell maintained, "God won't let it rain on Homecoming; He hasn't let it rain for sixteen years on Homecoming." The unbelieving reporters continued to question Falwell's faith. He replied, "We have spent $125,000 on this one meeting and God won't waste that money." Clouds threatened late Saturday night, but Sunday morning was a beautiful day. According to a visiting preacher, "God outdid Himself by creating a perfect day to preach out-of-doors." The crowd streamed in; sunglasses were everywhere. A few umbrellas were present but only as shade from the sun. The kids ran to sit on the grass near the platform on the north end of the football field. Workmen were busy behind the scene; everyone was busy and well organized: sound men, police directing traffic, over two hundred ushers, and maintenance men. At the last moment the movers arrived with the piano and organ from the church. Tuners worked briefly on the large grand piano and immediately the musicians began to play.

The people kept coming—3,128 of them—on the Sunday-school buses. The out of-state crowd was cut down because the national news media reported floods in Virginia, stating that roads were impassable. Phone calls came from Canada, South Carolina, and New York, asking if Lynchburg was accessible. They were told to come ahead, that only low-lying areas along rivers were flooded. Treasure Island, the church's camp, was under water; 240 beds where visitors were to sleep could not be used, and visitors had to go elsewhere. The dinner to be served on the grounds at Treasure Island had to be transferred to a local park. Falwell had set a goal of twenty thousand in Sunday school. A pastor from New York only brought twenty people in a Sunday-school bus; he had intended to bring fifty in two buses.

Jerry Falwell taught the Sunday-school lesson to everyone except the small children, who met back at Thomas Road Baptist Church. His lesson was on "saturation evangelism," and his text, Acts 2. Falwell believes the gospel should be preached to every available person by every available means at every available time. The massive crowd at Homecoming proved that his concept of evangelism is effective, and it is supported by *Christian Life* magazine's recognition last summer that Thomas Road is the fastest growing Sunday school in America.

Five TV color cameras were telecasting the service, one from eighty feet in a sky bucket. The 11:00 A.M. morning service was telecast over "The Old-Time Gospel Hour," seen over 206 stations throughout the United States. Falwell electrified the audience at the Lynchburg Stadium by announcing that he had signed a contract with an international network expanding "The Old-Time Gospel Hour" to 200 foreign stations around the free world. This qualifies Falwell as "the television pastor of the world."

The 11:00 A.M. service began with the television camera capturing a view of the Blue Ridge Mountains, the eternal background of Lynchburg, Virginia. Then the camera spanned the town of Lynchburg and finally zoomed in on the masses gathered in the stadium. The remote unit from Channel 3, WBT, Charlotte, North Carolina, relayed the morning service over microwaves to Akron, Ohio, where each Sunday "The Old-Time Gospel Hour" is videotaped, reproduced, and sent out to local stations.

Evangelist Bob Harrington, the Chaplain of Bourbon Street, spoke at the 11:00 A.M. service. Harrington gained fame preaching the gospel in the nightclubs of the French Quarter in New Orleans. Colonel Sanders of Kentucky Fried Chicken came and said, "A man is never too old to serve God." Sanders indicated that when he retired at age sixty-five, he went into the franchise business. At age seventy-eight, Sanders accepted Christ as his personal Saviour. He went on to explain that a man is never too old to start over. He had begun a new business and a new life, late in life.

Special music for both Sunday school and the morning service was supplied by Connie Smith, of Nashville, Tennessee, "the sweetheart of country-western singers." She admitted without apology to the crowd that when she first went to Nashville, she wanted a Cadillac and a hit recording. But these didn't satisfy her. God was speaking to her, and since her tender heart made her cry easily, she stopped attending church. After a religious TV special, a minister spoke to her of Jesus Christ. She wept unashamedly in front of producers and cameramen as she received Jesus Christ.

Doug Oldham, the weekly soloist for "The Old-Time Gospel Hour" presented his well-known rendition of "The King Is Coming." The Gethsemane Quartet of Greensboro, North Carolina, also sang.

Bob Harrington preached on the need for men to stand for God. At the end of his message, he challenged, "I want men to take their stand for God. I want every man willing to stand for God to come and stand before this pulpit." The muscular 250-pound evangelist continued his appeal, "If you are willing to have a family altar, to lead your family to church, to be a soul winner, to stand against cursing, to stand against vulgarity, to stand against smoking, to stand against booze, to stand against illicit sex, come if you are willing to take a stand for God."

Over six thousand men came and stood for God. Harrington had them kneel on the playing turf with heads bowed and committed the men to God.

Jerry Falwell came to close the meeting and testified how he received Christ in Lynchburg over twenty years ago. He wept unashamedly. Few of the associate pastors could remember seeing Falwell cry in the pulpit.

After the benediction there was a massive traffic jam. All the bus children were given "finger-lickin' good" fried chicken to eat on the bus ride home. Many of the guests were treated to dinner on the grounds of a local park.

A SECOND PENTECOST

Homecoming marked the beginning of the annual Pastors' and Workers' Conference held at Thomas Road Baptist Church. Over

five thousand delegates from almost every state in the union, repre-
senting almost every denomination, came for four days of instruction and inspiration. Every motel room within fifty miles was taken.
The concept of "Saturation Evangelism" gripped the delegates.
Hundreds of pastors came to the altar for spiritual commitment.
Every minister was challenged to go home and double his Sunday
school by January 1973; eight hundred pastors stood as a promise
that they would attempt to double their attendance.

When one visiting pastor saw the response of the pastors and
heard about the television expansion around the world, he exclaimed, "This is a second Pentecost, and the spread of evangelism
will be carried out by independent Baptist churches!"

The Pastors' and Workers' Conference was not a "how to" conference, but the seminars emphasized "how we did it." The eighty
workshops conducted by the staff of Thomas Road Baptist Church
emphasized the various ministries: television, radio, prison ministry, IBM computer, the pastoral staff, Sunday-school teaching
methods, the church business manager, mailings, Christian schools,
alcoholic ministry, youth work, Sunday-school busing, soul winning,
Junior Church, and many others.

Church growth was emphasized; the ten pastors of the ten
churches in the book *America's Fastest Growing Churches* preached
to the delegates and taught seminars. One delegate reflected, "Never
has so much expertise on church growth been assembled in one
spot."

A GREAT CHURCH CAMPUS

Thomas Road Baptist Church has $12 million invested in build-
ings and equipment spread over several hundred acres, yet the
church is more than mortar, bricks, and property. A great church is
vision, and Jerry Falwell announced in the spring of 1972 that the
church was moving to a new location on Candlers Mountain and
U.S. Route 29 Bypass. A great church is reflected in large buildings

and adequate space for expansion. The expansion master plan already includes two hundred acres, and Falwell is negotiating for additional acreage nearby. The Virginia Highway Commission is planning a new expressway on the south edge of the new property that will give added access to the church. A new ten-thousand-seat auditorium will sit on a hill and will be seen from most parts of Lynchburg. Parking is planned for forty-six hundred cars, and Sunday-school space is being designed by Lyles, Bissett, Carlisle and Wolff, Alexandria, Virginia, for twenty thousand pupils. The college accommodations will reach seven thousand and the high school will handle five thousand students. In addition, plans are being correlated on the new property for senior citizens' homes, orphanages, a computer center, a print shop to turn out 10 million pieces annually, plus office and administration space for all the ministries of Thomas Road Baptist Church.

According to Bob Hill of *Christian Life* magazine, this will be the largest church sanctuary in the history of Christianity. One observer noted that Thomas Road Baptist Church is providing all the ministries usually found at the denomination level. The strength of its program is in the local church laymen-oriented ministry. Many denominations have lost touch with the common man and have bogged down with institutional bureaucracy. Thomas Road Baptist Church is a local church, and all of the ministries are under a pastor who leads the people in soul winning, tithing, Bible study, and prayer.

THE FUTURE IS BRIGHT

Last year the largest Sunday school assembled at First Baptist Church, Hammond, Indiana, when 12,400 people attended on December 12, 1971. Those critics who predict the death of Sunday schools must be journalists who sit behind desks and read reports. Mark Twain once stated, "The news of my death is greatly exaggerated." Those who think the Sunday school is dying are wrong. They definitely have not visited Thomas Road Baptist Church. As of this printing, one of the largest Sunday schools since Pentecost met at Thomas Road Baptist Church. But there are hundreds of superaggressive pastors in independent Baptist churches who are building fast-growing churches. One of these days, perhaps one of them will have a larger attendance. Falwell replies, "I hope many beat our record of 19,020, because we are going to break that record and keep growing for God. I think the church will average 20,000 each Sunday, if present programs continue. The college will add 7,000 students and each of these will be involved in the church as soul winners, bus workers, and Sunday-school teachers. One thousand teachers, staff, and family will also attend Thomas Road Baptist Church." Falwell plans to have 2,000 in the senior citizens' home; they also will attend the church, as will the 1,000 in the orphanage. The Sunday school averaged 5,622 in 1972, with the college enrolling 305 students. When the college expands, along with the other growing ministries, Thomas Road Baptist Church can easily average 20,000 in Sunday school by the end of this decade, qualifying it as a miracle church.

2

PUTTING IT ALL TOGETHER

Jerry Falwell teaches the pastor's large adult class in the main sanctuary each Sunday morning, averaging approximately two thousand in attendance. Sometimes five thousand gather to hear him teach the Word of God; off Sundays the attendance dips embarrassingly low. At the end of his class, he gives an invitation for the unsaved to come to Jesus Christ. Always there are several who come forward seeking salvation. At the end of the invitation, Jerry hastens off the platform to the TV studio; it's 10:56 A.M.—four minutes to air time. The morning service of Thomas Road Baptist Church is televised under the name "The Old-Time Gospel Hour." The crew of twelve dedicated laymen are at their places ready to televise the morning service. Falwell usually makes them nervous by rushing into the studio at the last moment. The morning service is televised from the main sanctuary of the Thomas Road Baptist Church and relayed over microwaves to Akron, Ohio, where videotapes are made. These masters are in turn duplicated and sent out over America and the world to over four hundred stations.

"Two minutes to air time!" yells Tom Morrison, producer and director, over the headset, as Jerry Falwell rushes into the small room to put on makeup. The camera begins televising the place cards giving time, date, and program number. "Thirty seconds to air time." Couples stop Jerry to shake his hand as he goes into the studio. He takes a seat and hooks up his microphone just as Tom Morrison announces, "Ten seconds to air time." The cameraman's hand goes down. "Hello, I'm Jerry Falwell. I'd like you to stay tuned to 'The Old-Time Gospel Hour'."

Those four minutes between Sunday school and church are important preparation to put it all together. Four short minutes between Sunday school and the morning service—yet crucial in presenting the gospel to the world.

This chapter will take you approximately four minutes to read. It is composed of snapshots of Thomas Road Baptist Church. Since the ministry is difficult to describe in words, these anecdotes will give you glimpses into the working of God at Thomas Road. Just as a picture is worth a thousand words, so these short glimpses will help you catch the spirit and *feel* what God is doing. This chapter is designed to put Thomas Road Baptist Church together in your thinking.

Another book, *Church Aflame,* by Elmer Towns and Jerry Falwell, describes in detail the ministry of Thomas Road Baptist Church, giving illustrations of changed lives and how the ministry works in lives. Also, "how we did it" principles are included to help church workers build a superaggressive church. But perhaps you would be too busy to read an entire book; therefore, we have kept each story in this book short to help you view the total ministry of the church. On the other hand, some of you might think we spend too much time on these small details. These short snapshots may be like exploding fireworks on a dark summer evening, each giving a momentary picture. Even though they are short, viewed together they will help you understand the ministry of Thomas Road Baptist Church.

GAINING RESPECT FOR THE OUTREACH

One prayer meeting evening, a shabby-looking stranger sat on the steps between the church sanctuary and the academy building. His unshaven face was buried in his hands in apparent despair. Thomas Road had been advertised as a place where the rich, the

middle class, and the down-and-out could come worship God and
those who were unsaved could find Him. This man had heard the
reputation of Thomas Road Baptist Church and its care for the alcoholic, the poor, the needy, so he had come. Tom Diggs, a freshman at Lynchburg Baptist College, walked up and asked, "What's
wrong, sir?"

"Oh, I don't know," the man halfheartedly mumbled, and he ap-
parently wished to be left alone to find a solution to his problems in
the bottle tucked under his arm. Even though prayer meeting was
about to start, Tom saw that the man needed help and sat down beside him, placing his hand on the shoulder of the man's tattered
coat.

"Wouldn't you like to talk about it?" asked the kind student. The
man seemed shocked that anyone would care to talk to him. Tom
took his Bible and opened it up, presenting God's plan of salvation.
The man listened intently and said he understood what was being
explained, but was not ready to accept Christ.

Tom felt that a full stomach might make him a more ready lis-
tener. He was about to offer a meal when he saw Jerry Falwell
making his way to the auditorium for the prayer meeting service.
Tom called Falwell over to where the two were sitting. Falwell
spoke briefly with the man about the love of God. He directed Tom
and the shabby visitor to an associate pastor who would deal with
the man further. Falwell also indicated, "Bring the man over to the
service and I will talk with him after prayer meeting."

Tom hurried to find one of the staff members but when he returned a few minutes later, the stranger was gone. Deeply concerned about the needy soul, Tom began searching and finally spot-
ted him sitting in a car. Once more the young freshman pleaded
with the man to accept Christ but he simply said, "No," and pulled
away. Returning to the church auditorium, Tom met a friend who
had seen the encounter and had gone inside to pray for the man's
salvation.

The following day the phone rang in Pastor Falwell's office. The voice at the other end informed the secretary, "I am a seminary professor from Texas who is fully satisfied that the Thomas Road Baptist Church is indeed a 'church aflame.'" The man continued that he believed there was love and compassion in the church for the down-and-out as well as for the rich, because a young man had shown the love of Jesus Christ to a dirty, forsaken man the previous evening. The voice continued, "I know that the Thomas Road Baptist Church cares about derelicts because I was that man." Several weeks later the following letter was received by Dr. Falwell:

Dear Dr. Falwell:

Some time ago I had the privilege of visiting your church on Wednesday evening. I called your secretary the next morning and explained to her why I had come to the church grounds as a dirty bum with a wine bottle in my hands rather than with my customary suit and tie. I left there praising the Lord that somebody in your church would have cared for that kind of man and would have made a determined effort to reach him for Christ. The dear young man who talked to me was so persistent, so interested in me that I barely got away in time to get to my motel, clean myself up and get back for Prayer Meeting.

I want to thank you for leading a church to a place of keen concern for lost people. I have a deep respect and admiration for your ministry.

Devotedly yours,

Roy J. Fish, Th.D.
Professor of Evangelism
Southwestern Theological Seminary
Fort Worth, Texas

WATCHING THE BUSES COME IN

At 9:30 A.M. Sunday morning, just fifteen minutes before Sunday school starts, the Sunday-school buses begin arriving at Thomas Road Baptist Church. The Sunday-school bus director meets each bus, shouts a word of encouragement to the driver, and registers the number on the bus for that day. The buses begin parking to the rear of the lot and by the time they have all arrived over sixty-five buses have occupied a huge slice of the parking lot. One visitor mused as he visited Thomas Road Baptist Church for the first time, "I drove into the parking lot with extra time before Sunday school began. I wanted to look around and see how things operate. As soon as I got out of my car, I had to start dodging the buses as they arrived." Another visitor joked, "Make sure your insurance is paid when you come to Thomas Road—you might get run over by a bus, there are so many." Not all of the buses are bright school-bus yellow—some are green, some are blue, and others are a dirty yellow left over from public school days.

The buses begin leaving the church at 8:00 A.M. Sunday morning, some running eighty miles away to pick up Sunday-school pupils to bring them to Thomas Road Baptist Church. Adults as well as children ride the buses. Kids wave out windows and play in the back seats of the bus. Whatever they do, they are always noisy. They don't step out of the bus, they jump and hit the ground running, scattering in all directions toward Sunday school. With such a large number of riders, complete discipline is almost impossible. A few (not many) will run behind the buses and smoke, while some (once again, not many) will sneak up to the local grocery store and drink pop. The ushers go after them and try to persuade them to attend Sunday school. No children are ever physically harmed or dragged to Sunday school.

Where the buses disembark, some would think there is confusion because of the hundreds of people going in several directions. But people know where they are going. There are cars dodging buses, people dodging cars, kids dodging ushers. In the midst of the crowd are several young children holding large signs that read, "Follow me to the second-grade girls' Sunday-school class." "Or "Fourth-grade boys attend the Tree-House—follow me." Some of the children who come with parents for the first time do not try to find their age-grade Sunday-school class, but attend the pastor's Bible class in the sanctuary where Jerry Falwell teaches the Word of God. The staff is aware that children are in the pastor's class but many children are too frightened to be separated from their parents in such a large church the first time they visit. However, after having visited the church two or three times, most children will go with the ushers or others of their own class.

If there is confusion before Sunday school starts, nothing compares to the swarm of two thousand restless, screaming children leaving Junior Church running to the buses on the parking lot. Usually there is some treat waiting for them: candy, Kool-Aid, hamburgers, or some other novelty. Most children don't ride the bus because of the incentive, but the incentive helps create excitement about going to Thomas Road Baptist Church.

On Saturday morning, the work of Sunday-school buses gets done. The morning begins with coffee, doughnuts, and prayer. Next, drivers and workers are given a challenge and they are off to visit for the day. As they leave, promotional material is passed out, and the pockets of the drivers are filled with bubble gum. Every bus worker should be well liked by the children up and down the streets of Lynchburg and nearby areas. Many of the bus workers spend the rest of the day knocking on doors, talking to people about Jesus Christ. From the big expensive homes on Rivermont Avenue to the trailer courts on Campbell Avenue, the bus workers scatter to the end of Lynchburg and beyond, telling others about Jesus Christ and inviting them to ride the bus to Thomas Road Baptist Church.

THE TELEVISION CONTROL ROOM

Three stories above the auditorium floor is a large plate-glass window. Behind it is the television studio of "The Old-Time Gospel Hour." Tom Morrison, director of "The Old-Time Gospel Hour," sits at the consoles and, with headphones, he is connected to each cameraman, engineer, and director. Through the electronic miracle of television, Tom puts "The Old-Time Gospel Hour" into the homes of millions each week.

Thirty minutes before the program begins, he says, "Good morning," greeting his cameramen as he brings each microphone alive. The four cameramen, their assistants, and the other engineer on the consoles begin following his orders.

Dusty Rhodes is producer and engineer for "The Old-Time Gospel Hour." Dusty Rhodes's brains and continued determination have put together the television and radio studio. According to Jerry Falwell, "Dusty is responsible for putting us on the stations each week." He is a full-time engineer for General Electric in Lynchburg, but his greatest delight is working in the TV studio at Thomas Road Baptist Church. Dusty takes all of the crises in stride and smiles with his usual "Let's remember we're involved in some important business."

Not all of the men and women who help to televise "The Old-Time Gospel Hour" have been professionally trained. Yet, all have gone through enough training with Tom Morrison and Dusty Rhodes that their enthusiasm and willingness has earned them the title "professional." Each week there is a certain tenseness—it's not uneasiness, yet it's a sense that they are serving God and influencing millions of lives.

"The Old-Time Gospel Hour" is not a produced show from a television studio. Rather, television adapts its cameras and technical production for the Sunday-morning service. Jerry Falwell is of the opinion that "The Old-Time Gospel Hour" should not be a production, as these shows lack spiritual vitality. Rather, Falwell believes the TV cameras should attempt to capture the preaching and movement of God as He works in hearts at the Thomas Road Baptist Church. This is why the cameras focus on those coming forward, to show what God is doing in lives.

Tom Morrison sits in the control booth; four monitors tell him what the four cameras are viewing. The first may be on Jerry's face, the second on a grandmother flipping through her Bible, the third capturing the entire pulpit, and the fourth, a slide announcement. With precision and sensitivity, Tom changes from the close-up view of Jerry Falwell preaching to the grandmother pointing a shriveled finger at a Scripture verse; later Tom changes to a larger picture of the entire platform, showing Falwell as he moves to the right side of the pulpit.

Emergencies sometimes happen while the program is being televised. One Sunday a television tube blew out in number 2 camera and Dusty Rhodes quickly ran to the small studio, tore down number 4 camera, took the tube and replaced it in the main camera, and had it functioning before the service was over. Other minor problems for the crew such as dead microphones, changing color according to sunlight in the auditorium, and Bob Harrington who walks all over the platform, keep the television technicians on their toes. But they get deep satisfaction out of the many letters read each Wednesday evening at prayer meeting by Jerry Falwell. Of the thousands of letters that come in each day, Jerry reads several each prayer meeting telling of outstanding testimonies of those who have found Christ by watching "The Old-Time Gospel Hour." These testimonies keep Dusty, Tom, and the crew coming back on their off evenings to repair equipment, set up backdrops, and keep "The Old-Time Gospel Hour" on the air.

A MASTER TEACHER AT WORK

The fourth-grade boys have an exciting Sunday-school class at Thomas Road Baptist Church. At 8:30 on Sunday morning teacher Bill Newton, former Oregon highway patrolman, can be found on the second floor of the Carter building preparing his classroom for the invasion of ninty nine-year-old boys. The class is decorated as The Tree House Club. First, a six-foot fence (logs painted on plywood) is put up around the door to simulate an entrance to a tree house. An eight-foot painted cardboard tree stands outside the fence to add atmosphere. Next, Newton places signs around the Sunday-school building, directing any new fourth-grade boy to the Tree House. By 9:15 the boys start arriving in buses and in cars. By 10:00 A.M., ninety boys are packed into the classroom, which is public-school size, used by Lynchburg Christian Academy during the week.

Nine months ago muscular Bill took over the class and greeted eleven boys. He was determined to have the largest class in the Sunday School. The challenge of teaching in America's fastest growing Sunday school encouraged Bill to build a class proportionate to the Sunday school. His wife, Sharon, acts as secretary and teacher.

Promotions and special days excited the boys to bring their friends. The greatest excitement surrounded the boys' receiving play money for attendance, memorizing verses, and bringing guests. A yo-yo champion, the barefoot hillbilly preacher, and a karate exhibition were other promotions used to attract unsaved boys to class. Soon the class was averaging forty-five boys, more than Bill and his wife could handle. Bill states, "We then went into team teaching, with the help of three Lynchburg Baptist College students." Bill feels that combining the talents of several teachers gives more continuity to the class. Storytelling, song leading, and discipline are now shared by the team.

Weekly highlights that hold the boys' interest include a skit by the Nutty Professor (one of the teachers). The "professor" teaches Bible truths, especially those counteracting evolution, through stories. The boys are quizzed about the previous weeks' lessons. Each time they answer correctly, they hang a piece of a four-foot dummy of the devil in place. When Satan is hanged, the boys yell because they have defeated him.

A weekly newspaper, *Fourth Grade Express,* is mailed to each boy. The paper has a prayer list, a Bible story, and promotional information. Bill says, "Boys think with their hands, feet, and voices and it's important to have an action-oriented class." He further states, "Promotion will get the boys into the class but won't keep them coming week after week. Good Bible teaching is the answer. Get them saved and then feed them from God's Word and you'll have boys excited about Sunday school."

To help his boys learn the gospel, Newton uses the *Wordless Book* with its black, red, white, and gold pages. The boys are led to the Lord, then they are taught how to lead other boys to Christ. One hundred and twenty-two boys have made salvation decisions in the first nine months. This is enough reason for Newton to expect bigger and better things in the future.

JUNIOR CHURCH

Each Sunday morning approximately two thousand boys and girls, ages six through twelve, crowd into the gymnasium at 11:00 A.M. for Junior Church. The former bus director of the Thomas Road Baptist Church was also Sunday-morning preacher for this congregation of juniors. His enthusiastic song leading got them clapping their hands, shouting "Amen" and, on one particular chorus, stomping their feet. However, all of the singing is not gospel ditties or choruses. He believed that church for children should be similar to an adult service. They should sing hymns, have special music, read the Scriptures, and hear gospel preaching. The director was very specific that the message should not be a flannelgraph story or another Bible lesson. He preached the gospel to the juniors. He stated, "God has blessed preaching in the church and children need gospel preaching."

Nevertheless, he put the sermon on their level. Children were exhorted, admonished, and motivated to serve God. This director believed that children identify with the heroes of the Bible. He usually chose a story centered around a great hero of the faith. He stated, "Children identify with great men of God and want to live lives like them." He went on to state that children too often have heroes in the world, movies and politics. Among his favorite sermons were Samson, David and Goliath, and Joshua and the walls of Jericho.

To the casual observer at Junior Church, it was apparent that that director had become a hero to his congregation. While acting out David and Goliath, he removed his partial plate, ruffled his hair, and growled the part of a giant. In his preaching he used object lessons—a giant's spear, an actual sword, or whatever it took to make the children pay attention to the Word of God. He stated, "You've got to make these stories come alive to the kids; it is the Word of God that prepares their hearts. It's my job to present the Bible in as exciting a manner as possible."

Each week a fun time allows the kids to yell, laugh, and applaud. One week a leader swallowed a live goldfish because his bus children had broken an attendance record by bringing visitors on the buses. Another time, a driver let the boys and girls honey and feather him in the parking lot. The obvious excitement over the good-natured fun communicated itself to the children: "We enjoy attending the Thomas Road Baptist Church." Junior Church workers believe that if children enjoy attending church, they will bring their friends to hear the Word of God. Those who hear the leaders teach the Word of God to children or present the plan of salvation to a lost person know they are serious teachers of the Word, and are earnest soul winners. No one can ever accuse them of being frivolous with the gospel.

Each Sunday a number of children respond to the invitation to be saved. One Sunday there were ten, while a different week there were over fifty boys and girls coming down the aisle. Each child is talked with personally to make sure he knows why he is coming, then dealt with by a counselor who shows from the Bible how to be saved. The end of Junior Church coincides with the morning service of Thomas Road Baptist Church. The children who come forward are then brought into the main sanctuary and led down the aisle. According to Falwell, "Those children coming forward are a testimony to the adults in the main service that God is working in every area of Thomas Road Baptist Church." Falwell continued, "Some people think it is unsophisticated to have children walk down an aisle, but they have eternal souls and when they sincerely respond to Jesus Christ, God saves them."

Do the children like Junior Church? "Sure—I haven't missed a Sunday this year," responded one. "Are you saved?" "Uh huh," the second one said. "I went forward and received the Lord last week."

INVITATION TIME

There is a hush over the entire sanctuary as the sermon reaches its climax. Jerry asks the thousands before him to bow their heads and close their eyes. "Would those of you who have accepted Christ as Saviour raise your hand in thanksgiving? Thank you." As Pastor Falwell speaks these words, the other pastors of Thomas Road Baptist Church silently walk to the front of the main sanctuary and stand before the congregation with bowed heads.

Falwell pleads with the audience, "Those of you who could not raise your hand, be honest and lift your hand indicating, 'Jerry, I've never really been born again. Please pray for me.' " There is a show of hands as people respond. Falwell continues, "There are some of you who are saved, but your life doesn't show it; if you'll raise your hand before God, I'll pray for you, too."

From the large white rectangular pulpit Dr. Falwell prays, "O God, help people do *today,* what they will be glad they have done when they stand before the judgment seat." He continues to ask for a visitation from heaven by God's Holy Spirit, which will result in a harvest of souls.

"If you have not come to know Jesus Christ as personal Saviour, and you would like to receive Him, walk down the aisle and take the hand of one of our pastors. He'll show you to a personal worker who will open the Word of God and show you His plan of salvation." For fifteen years or more, these words at the close of every service have always resulted in a harvest of souls. The seeds of the gospel are spread daily by the spiritually-minded congregation, but the harvest is most often seen at the close of one of the three weekly services.

As the invitation is given, trained personal workers, Bibles in hand, start down the aisles. Almost as soon as they arrive at the front, they meet someone to counsel.

Gray-haired women, with work-worn hands grasping tattered Bibles, place arms around young girls. Other ladies lead elderly women gently down the stairs to the counseling room.

In the counseling room, folding chairs have been placed in groups of two. Soon they are filled with seeking souls and prayerful soul winners.

In one set of chairs can be seen a young high-school athlete sincerely talking with a teammate. Next to him may be seen graying heads bowed in rededication. Maybe a couple of veteran factory workers have decided to begin life anew.

As the chairs fill up, soul winners and seekers can be seen lowering to their knees as they begin to turn the pages of their Bibles.

About halfway through the invitation, the wide central doors at the back of the sanctuary slowly swing open. In march twenty or thirty boys and girls who moments earlier heard the gospel in Junior Church and now come to be saved. Down the aisle they come, in age from four or five up to ten or twelve. Many walk with heads bowed, but most look up long enough to flash a grin at Pastor Falwell as they pass the pulpit.

As the congregation and choir sing the chorus "Harvest Time," Pastor Falwell makes his final plea to the congregation in front of him. He asks the people to be seated and from either door of the counseling room come ushers with small yellow decision cards.

For the soul winners and Jerry Falwell, this moment is the reward for their prayers and witnessing. He takes the small yellow cards, and with a smile begins to read them:

"Mr. and Mrs. Joe Thompson come for salvation, baptism, and church membership.

"Bonnie Baker comes submitting for baptism.

"A whole family comes for salvation. Amen. The Jim Kennedy family.

"Dave Gehman comes for rededication, baptism, and church membership.

"Jerry Walker comes for salvation. Amen.

"Amen."

"I WAS IN PRISON, AND YE CAME UNTO ME"

An irritating odor from the open toilets and a heavy smell of smoke from the many burning cigarettes greeted the visitor as he walked into cell block six. Everything was painted gray, except the large white splotches on the walls where the paint had long since peeled off. A worn-out checkerboard and a frayed deck of cards lay on the small metal bench in the open area in front of the five eight-foot-square cells in the block. The three black men and four white men inside the cell block cocked their heads to get a glimpse of the outsider who had disturbed their foreboding and sometimes hopeless world. In the dim light they could see a man. He wasn't a cop, and he didn't look like a lawyer. Just who was he?

"Hi! I'm Reverend Ed Martin," came the cheerful voice of the visitor. The prisoners stopped wondering, and four of the inmates jumped down from their bunks and ambled over to where Mr. Martin was standing outside the bars. They cautiously eyed the preacher as he reached through the bars to shake their hands. They were suspicious of everyone, preachers included.

"I'm ex-Virginia convict number 46362," began Ed Martin. "I broke rocks while shackled on a Virginia chain gang over twenty-eight years ago, and I'd like to leave you my story, *The Man Who Broke Rocks.*"

The ice was broken; he could talk to them openly now. They had dropped their walls of resistance against the outside world. He was in, because Ed Martin had once stood where they stood now—behind bars.

Saved on a Virginia chain gang in 1944, Ed Martin has, since 1965, devoted his entire life to prison evangelism, reaching and preaching behind iron bars to the thousands of men, women, and juveniles that fill America's prisons. For fifteen years prior to 1965, Ed and his wife, Alfreda, were missionaries in Japan, but Ed Martin's concern for an evangelistic outreach to convicts grew until he was forced to return to America and start such a ministry. After much prayer and hard work, Hope Aglow Ministry, Incorporated, was established in Lynchburg as a home mission outreach of the fast-growing Thomas Road Baptist Church.

Today, Hope Aglow is headquartered at 209 Madison Avenue, Lynchburg, but it is still an integral part of the Thomas Road church. Brother Martin has traveled in forty-six states preaching in the prisons and reaching convicts with the saving message of Jesus Christ. In addition to Ed's travels throughout America, he and his wife and two other staff members spend many long hours corresponding with prisoners. A free Bible correspondence course is offered to any prisoner who would like to enroll. Over one thousand men and women are presently enrolled in the courses, with many saved as a direct result. Brother Martin praises God for the miracles that have been wrought thus far and looks forward to continued expansion of the ministry.

INTO THE HIGHWAYS AND BYWAYS GO THE BUS WORKERS

The Sunday-school bus ministry has the greatest potential for evangelism in today's church. More souls are won to Jesus Christ and identified with local churches through Sunday-school busing than any other medium of evangelism. According to conservative estimates, approximately fifty are led to the Lord each week because of the Sunday-school bus ministry. Some of the most spectacular conversions come through Sunday-school bus contacts.

The bus director was visiting in Bedford County, twenty-seven miles from the church, with Jack Gillespie. They called at a rural farm home. The owner was a faithful member of a Methodist church and one of the leading officials. He indicated, "My church doesn't give me a chance to be saved." He went on to explain that the Methodist church did not give an invitation. The director responded, "I'll give you a chance to get saved today." He gave an invitation, even though only one person was present. After he presented the gospel, he asked the man to put his hand on the open Bible as an expression of his desire to be saved, then urged, "This is your chance." The farmer placed both big hands on the Bible and received Jesus Christ. He did not want to leave the Methodist church, but the visitor told him, "If you had cancer and went to a doctor who lied to you and did not help you get well, would you go back?" The man quickly replied, "It will take me one week to get rid of my responsibilities in the Methodist church." He has been at Thomas Road ever since.

The bus ministry is the evangelistic arm of the church, reaching into neighborhoods and bringing adults and children under the sound of the gospel. Workers in many places emphasize only children, but those at Thomas Road go after both children and adults. Last fall Falwell baptized eight couples one Sunday evening. Both fathers and mothers had been won to Jesus Christ.

Some bus ministries place primary emphasis on contests, trinkets, and awards for children to get them to ride the bus. The philosophy at Thomas Road has always been to motivate the workers. The primary objective is to get captains to reach children. The secondary objective is to work with the bus riders.

Many bus workers only work in the housing projects, ghetto areas, and among the poor in the slums. All people within a community must be reached, the poor as well as the affluent. Thomas Road Baptist Church has sixteen buses that operate in middle-class neighborhoods of twenty-five-thousand-dollar homes and above. One bus brings in thirty-five riders from the status Boonsboro district, while the next bus that unloads on Sunday morning is from the Greenfield Housing Project, and the bare feet and dirty clothes indicate a poverty level.

Lynchburg has only fifty-four thousand people and some feel the Sunday-school bus ministry has reached its saturation point. Now twenty-one buses leave the city limits and bring children in from rural areas and distant towns such as Bedford, Alta Vista, Appomattox, Amherst, and Thaxton. One reaches fifty miles to Roanoke.

The plan of reaching those around a church is biblical. "Go out quickly into the streets and lanes of the city, and bring in hither the poor, and the maimed, and the halt, and the blind. . . . Go out into the highways and hedges, and compel them to come in, that my house may be filled" (Luke 14:21,23). ". . . and ye shall be witnesses unto me both in Jerusalem, and in all Judea, and in Samaria, and unto the uttermost part of the earth" (Acts 1:8). Some churches are not growing because they are more concerned about the rest of

the world than about the children in their own neighborhood and
city. Paul was concerned about reaching the neighborhood. "And
how I kept back nothing that was profitable unto you, but have shew-
ed you, and have taught you publickly, and from house to house"
(Acts 20:20).

Why is God blessing the bus ministry? Because it is a program of
getting churches back to God's way of reaching people, which is
house-to-house, door-to-door witnessing. Most of the growing
churches in the United States have a bus ministry.

Bus work is hard work, but there is not another job in the church
that will result in a larger attendance for an equal amount of work
hours invested. Thomas Road Baptist Church maintains its bus
ministry by house-to-house surveys. The workers are instructed to
go to the home and ask the parents if they will allow their children
to ride the bus. Jerry Falwell maintains, "We begin by asking for
the child, but our ultimate aim is the entire family."

The bus workers meet at 9:00 A.M. on Saturday morning for
prayer, coffee, and fellowship. Within a half hour they are out on
the streets calling in homes. The average worker spends at least
three hours on Saturday visiting both his riders and new prospects.
The bus worker knocks on the door and introduces himself: "Hello
there, I am Joe Dokes from the Thomas Road Baptist Church. Our
church has a bus that comes through your area. Would you allow
your children to ride my bus to Sunday school?" Survey work is
simply a friendly invitation. Later, bus workers revisit the home, attempting to lead people to Jesus Christ.

How permanent is the work of the Sunday-school bus ministry?
A farmer who was reached by a Sunday-school bus now helps
on a bus for Thomas Road Baptist Church. He is also a soul
winner. He gave the name of his eighty-year-old uncle to Carrol
Ferguson, former assistant director of Thomas Road Baptist
Church bus ministry. This uncle was a murderer, recently released
from prison. Carrol Ferguson knew that Doug Hunt, student at

Lynchburg Baptist College, drives a Sunday-school bus in the Alta Vista area where the elderly ex-convict lives. Carrol and Doug called on him, inviting him to ride the bus. The conversation immediately drifted to spiritual matters.

"Can God forgive me for killing my brother?" the guilty man was anxious to know. Carrol Ferguson quietly opened God's Word and showed him that the blood of Jesus Christ cleanses from all sin. Doug Hunt's fervent "Amen" supported Carrol. The trio examined many verses showing the forgiveness of sin through faith in the shed blood of Jesus Christ. The elderly gentleman quietly placed his hand on the Bible to indicate his willingness to repent from sin. He bowed his head to tell God he was sorry. As the bus workers were leaving, the eighty-year-old new convert said, "I'll be there Sunday. Don't come down this lane—I'll walk up and catch the bus on the road."

MYTHS ABOUT THE OFFERING

An elderly couple entered Thomas Road Baptist Church and sat toward the rear of the auditorium. They were visitors and, after getting comfortable, the lady looked down and noticed the large offering plates and nudged her husband. "See, they don't use bushel baskets!" (The church actually uses salad bowls for offering plates.) Many unsaved people criticize the Thomas Road Baptist Church for its emphasis on the collection. One critic exclaimed that he wouldn't attend because all they wanted was money. Others believe the rumor that Falwell locks the doors during the offering, which is not true.

All visitors are asked to raise their hands and are given visitors' envelopes. Falwell points out from the pulpit, "We don't have you fill out visitors' *cards,* because you can't put money in a card." Almost everyone laughs.

Jerry Falwell believes the scriptural exhortation that "where your treasure is, there will your heart be also" (Matthew 6:21). By this he indicates, "If you get a man's pocketbook, you will eventually get his support." Falwell goes on to explain his emphasis on finances. "God commanded that all men tithe to the local church, and those who don't, rob God. If a Christian is not giving money to God, he is not obedient, and we teach Christians to be obedient by giving money." As the visitor glances around at the multi-million-dollar building, television, printing presses, and computer, he realizes it takes money to finance such an operation. Thomas Road Baptist Church is one of the most aggressive evangelistic churches in America because it puts a biblical emphasis on money. It continues to grow, because God blesses a church that gives sacrificially.

The money at Thomas Road Baptist Church stays in motion and, according to Falwell, "We are always broke." The money never sits in a bank account nor is it saved for a rainy day. "We use money to win souls for Jesus Christ," says Falwell.

The entire student body of Lynchburg Baptist College was taken to Israel during January, 1972, as part of their academic experience. This cost the college, and the church which underwrites the college, $55,800. But Falwell believes that, "There is that scattereth, and yet increaseth; and there is that withholdeth more than is meet, but it tendeth to poverty" (Proverbs 11:24). A number of visitors from other churches and faithful listeners to "The Old-Time Gospel Hour" came along on the tour. These Christians saw the zealous work of the students in winning souls to Jesus Christ. They witnessed to tour guides, bus drivers, and waiters. On Sunday morning in the Bay of Haifa, church was held aboard the luxury liner *Orpheus*. At the end of that service Falwell received an offering for the work of "The Old-Time Gospel Hour," Lynchburg Baptist College, and the other ministries of Thomas Road Baptist Church; $93,000 was received in cash and pledges that morning, proving that God blesses the financial outreach of a church that puts the right emphasis on money.

TRAVELING WITH JERRY

The bright orange sunset temporarily blinded the pilot as he banked the church-owned twin-engine Cessna 414 into the final approach pattern to the Akron-Canton, Ohio, air terminal. The plane was on flight to Lynchburg from Detroit, Michigan, where its passengers, Dr. Falwell and Dr. Towns, had spoken at the 1971 Michigan Sunday-School Teachers' Convention. A brief stop at the Akron-Canton terminal would allow disembarkation of the advertising agency executive in charge of the radio and television promotion of "The Old-Time Gospel Hour."

The plane shuddered slightly as the landing gear locked into place. The pilot took manual control of the red-and-white seven-passenger craft and prepared to swing the Cessna into line with several other approaching aircraft. Suddenly, the air traffic controller's voice boomed over the plane's radio telling the pilot, "Abort and fly off!" Seconds before, he had received permission for final approach; now the air controller told him to make another approach, flying a wide, circular pattern. Reluctantly, and a bit disgruntled, the pilot obeyed.

"Five-eight Quebec requesting final approach pattern clearance," barked the pilot into the mike as he came around for his second landing attempt. The landing gear locked into place once again as the air controller finished giving his instructions.

Harry Dean, a Lynchburg Baptist College student riding in the copilot's seat, was busily scanning the skies for any other aircraft that might hazard the landing. Not knowing how close other planes should come to his own, he asked the pilot to lean across the cockpit and see if an oncoming single-engine blue airplane presented any danger.

"There's one coming over the top of us!" yelled Dr. Falwell from the passenger compartment, as the pilot craned his head to see the other craft. He took one look at the fast-approaching aircraft and quickly banked the Cessna into a steep dive to avoid a mid-air collision. Anxious moments elapsed before the plane leveled off and continued its landing approach. The red and-white bird finally touched down, and the departing passengers happily set their feet on the ground.

Near misses, refueling stops, and air traffic controllers are a routine part of Dr. Falwell's life, for much of his traveling time is now spent flying to and from speaking engagements coast to coast. Falwell's rapidly expanding ministry forced the Thomas Road Baptist Church in the spring of 1971 to acquire a fully equipped, pressurized, $225,000 Cessna 414.

His many hours of flying time afford Jerry the opportunity to answer many of the thousands of letters that pour into the church offices weekly. When Dr. Towns, Dave Beaver, Doug Oldham, or other staff members accompany Jerry, the plane provides an ideal conference room to plan future developments of Thomas Road's various ministries.

Although the plane is a tremendous asset to Dr. Falwell and the church, he has experienced times when bicycling might accomplish more in the way of travel. In the fall of 1971, Jerry was returning to Lynchburg from Nashville, Tennessee, late one Saturday night, when a violent storm front forced the plane to land in Johnson City, Tennessee, at 3:00 A.M. Sunday morning. A determined Jerry phoned the manager of a local rent-a-car agency, waking him from a deep sleep, and asked him to come to the airport and rent him a car. After driving four hours, the sleepy-eyed pastor arrived in Lynchburg in time for the morning services at Thomas Road.

With the continuing rapid expansion of the ministries of Thomas Road and the new Lynchburg Baptist College, the church purchased a six-hundred-thousand-dollar Convair 580 in April, 1972. The thirty-two-passenger twin-turbo-engined plane is capable of flying nonstop coast to coast. The cabin is split into four compartments, two of which will convert into bedrooms.

George M. Fay was hired as the church's full-time pilot in December, 1971, and captains the new airship. George and his wife Diane are examples of the impact of the superaggressive ministry of Thomas Road Baptist Church. George, a resident of Lynchburg, was a successful nuclear engineer when first approached by a church staff member to be a standby pilot for Dr. Falwell. Although George and Diane were both saved and faithful church members at another Baptist church in Lynchburg, they lacked the real joy that comes from being surrendered, soul-winning Christians. Several flying trips with Jerry and several visits to services at Thomas Road soon changed their lives and their biblical stand for Jesus.

If time and distance allow, Dr. Falwell drives to many speaking engagements. His car's mobile telephone unit enables him to keep in constant contact with his staff and family. Several times an emergency contact on his car phone has enabled him to meet bereaved relatives at a hospital deathbed.

Dr. Falwell attempts to accomplish as much driving as he does flying, dictating letters or messages to his staff. Hours on the highway give him time to pray and to formulate plans for the church. While driving home from a speaking engagement in Richmond late one night he formulated the Doorkeeper and Faith Partner phases of "The Old-Time Gospel Hour." In our day of rapid transportation, Jerry Falwell uses every means possible to spread the gospel.

A TRIP TO THE HOLY LAND

Ninety-three students of Lynchburg Baptist College took a nine-day tour of Bible lands in January, 1972, led by Dr. Jerry Falwell, pastor of Thomas Road Baptist Church, and Dr. Elmer Towns, vice-president of the college. The entire student body in good standing was given an all-expenses-paid tour as part of the educational activity at the college.

The tour included four nations, with a jet flight from Richmond,

Virginia, to Nicosia, Cyprus. The students boarded the luxury liner *Orpheus* and traveled to biblical sites in Turkey, Syria, Lebanon, and Israel. Members from the church and friends from around America swelled the total tour group to 232.

The *Orpheus* became a floating classroom, hotel, and dining room, with Dr. Towns lecturing each evening on biblical backgrounds of the geographical sites to be visited the following day.

Dr. R. O. Woodworth, former executive vice-president of Baptist Bible College, Springfield, and one of the instructors on the trip, said, "Taking an entire student body to the Holy Land is the boldest move for a Christian college I have ever heard, and the instructional experience to the students will be an educative impact that cannot be measured in classroom time here in the States."

When asked about the expense, Dr. Falwell replied, "This trip is a down payment on our pledge that Lynchburg Baptist College will be the most outstanding college in America, giving quality education, local church evangelism, and training in Christian character." The cost of the trip was not hidden in the students' tuition, inasmuch as tuition is only one hundred fifty dollars per semester. This year the college will again be taking all of its students abroad. The author explained that students are reluctant to invest their freshman year of study in a new college because of many unknown factors, especially lack of accreditation. He went on to explain that the financial investments in this educational seminar, along with other similar innovations in quality educational experiences, are an indication of the administration's commitment to meet accreditation standards.

Early each morning, the students left the floating hotel to board buses and visit geographical sites of biblical significance. In Turkey they visited Tarsus, the home of Paul, and Antioch, the site of the first missionary church, where believers were first called Christians. In the ancient city of Damascus, Syria, they visited the scene of Paul's conversion and the ancient wall from which Paul made his escape from persecution.

Two days were spent in Galilee examining the boyhood home of Jesus Christ and the scenes of His ministry: Nazareth, Capernaum, Tiberias, and the Sea of Galilee. The ancient city of Jerusalem highlighted the tour, with visits to Calvary, the Garden of the Tomb, the Temple site, and the Mount of Olives. The entire student body took communion in the Garden of the Tomb.

Considerable time was spent in examining archaeological sites such as Jericho, Megiddo, Qumran, and the excavation of the west wall of the Temple. Lectures in archaeology were supplied by the Israeli Department of Tourism. Also, the ruins of the temple of Baalbek were visited in Lebanon. These students should have a better grasp of the Bible because of their trip abroad, and should be better soul winners because of their experience in Thomas Road Baptist Church.

MINISTRY TO THE ALCOHOLIC

In January of 1959, a farm in Appomattox County was opened up to twelve men for spiritual help. Although the work has been relocated, it has been operating regularly ever since that time. This is the Elim Home for Alcoholics, a ministry of the Thomas Road Baptist Church. Mr. and Mrs. Ray Horsley, directors, felt a need to minister to these men who have a problem with which Mr. Horsley was only too familiar himself.

"We believe that alcoholism is not a disease, but is simply a sin," says Mr. Horsley. "This is what the Bible teaches; and there is only one remedy—the blood of Jesus Christ." Elim Home stands on God's Word and all the men that come to the home are taught it. "We teach that Jesus Christ is the only answer," explained Mr. Horsley. "We offer no medical services and our doctor is only called for emergencies."

The eighteen men that live in the new home in Amherst County are all there of their own free will. No one gets put in. Each man must agree to stay at least sixty days for help. "We feel we need at least this much time to teach each man the things he must know concerning his new life in Christ." The rule is that a man must come completely sober, although exceptions have been made. No one is allowed any alcoholic beverages while residing in the home.

The men live two in a room with paneled walls and carpeted floors. There are group devotions every morning after breakfast and then the men go their ways. A few work outside the home, often at Thomas Road Baptist Church. The men, who are all different ages, take care of the home. "Mrs. Horsley likes the way we keep house," one man said. The men rotate jobs and do a little of everything. A few of the men even do the cooking. But everyone helps do the dishes.

The men pay nothing for their stay and they remain as long as there is a need. The whole home boards a bus for Sunday and Wednesday night church services at Thomas Road Baptist Church. Attendance is mandatory.

Almost every man has a hobby, and visitors are always impressed with the talent of the men. Every evening there is a chapel service in the main hall, and often outside groups will come in to conduct the program. For years, Mr. Davis's Sunday-school class at Thomas Road Baptist Church has been giving the program at least once a month and then the ladies provide refreshments.

NINETEEN TEEN-AGERS HELP BUILD A CHURCH IN OLD MEXICO

Nineteen teen-agers from the Thomas Road Baptist Church invested ten days in Monterrey, Mexico, as summer missionaries in June, 1971, reaching Mexicans for Christ. In five working days they actually constructed *Baptisto Templo,* a Baptist church, and left 417 Mexican believers who had professed faith in Jesus Christ.

The young people joined 230 other teen-agers from independent Baptist churches in Riverdale, Maryland, Huntington, West Virginia, and Kansas City, Missouri, for an intensive saturation of the suburbs of Monterrey with the gospel.

Church buses conveyed the teens to Mexico, where the American young people learned foreign missions by actually performing evangelism in a foreign culture. The Reverend Lonnie Smith, missionary under the Baptist Bible Fellowship, directs Camp Rio Escondido, located in the Sierra Madre Mountains. Each summer over one thousand American teen-agers are quartered at the camp. Each day the teen-agers spread out into mountain villages, ranchos on the plains, and the suburbs of metropolitan Monterrey to win Mexicans to Christ.

Each teen-ager secured thirty American sponsors back home to donate one dollar each, which purchased three Spanish New Testaments. The youth group was divided into three sections. One third of the kids distributed New Testaments in the neighborhoods and invited people to an evangelistic service. A second third did the manual labor in construction of the Baptist church. The final third remained at the camp for the necessary housekeeping chores. The Thomas Road kids distributed twenty thousand New Testaments during the week. Debbie Towns testified, "We waded through mud up to our knees to hand out Bibles, yet it was worth it to see their smiles." A total of 417 people were saved in their services, and twenty-eight of the American kids surrendered for full-time Christian service. Doreen Ingalls testified, "I was saved but not dedicated. When I saw the hundreds of little children, they moved my heart to want to serve Christ." She is registered at Lynchburg Baptist College.

Early each morning, the school buses were jammed with young missionaries leaving the camp to evangelize a local hamlet or colony (the word for neighborhood). No cameras were allowed because the kids were workers, not tourists. Arriving at a colony, two American youths were paired with a Mexican interpreter, and went door to door placing Bibles in the homes. The American teens were sur-

rounded by children begging for Bibles, but Lonnie Smith directed
the high schoolers: "Do not distribute the Bibles in the street. Place
them in the homes." Everyone was invited to an evangelistic service
that evening. The American youth choir sang and a visiting youth
pastor spoke through an interpreter.

The summer missionary experience gave American teens a new
appreciation for money, home and educational facilities back home.
Joyce Lockhart testified, "I want to thank God I'm an American."

Before the teen-agers left for Monterrey, Thomas Road Baptist
Church raised twelve hundred dollars to build the Baptist church
(twenty-five by forty-six feet). Because of the overwhelming success, Missionary Smith added an eighteen-by-thirty-six-foot Christian
education wing, which cost an extra three thousand dollars. After
the teen-agers returned and gave their testimonies in the Thomas
Road Baptist Church, Jerry Falwell asked for additional finances to
help pay one thousand dollars toward the cost of the wing. Immediately adults and teen-agers stood across the auditorium, some
pledging twenty-five dollars, others ten dollars, and some one dollar, meeting the goal.

The high-school boys arrived at the work site at 5:00 A.M. each
morning and worked until the afternoon sun was unbearable. Mark
Carderelli testified that they could never have built the church and
its educational wing in five working days without prayer. An American foreman who directed the boys indicated it would have taken
union labor two months to finish the project. Carderelli described
an approximate crowd of five hundred children who stood to watch
them work each day, while old men sat in the shade and watched.
"Jose, a little boy, kept trying to steal our wallets, but we loved
him." Young Carderelli testified, "My greatest thrill was seeing Jose
apologize with tears on the last night, after he had accepted Jesus."

The church is no chicken coop. Steve Reaves testifies of breaking
rock, mixing concrete, and laying cement block. "We prayed that
building up." Construction was hampered because for the first time

in recent history rain poured on the high-school laborers. On the evening of June 22, the kids arrived for the dedication of the building to find over 900 people waiting to get into the auditorium, which seated 200. The youth choir sang, the Reverend Truman Dollar (pastor, Kansas City Baptist Temple) preached, and 147 people received Christ. Reaves said, "Thomas Road Baptist Church is growing fast, but our church in Mexico began in one day with 175 conversions." Missionary Smith has begun twenty-seven churches in his last sixteen years in Mexico.

Anne Mason, a freshman at Lynchburg Baptist College, explained, "I learned God can do anything." Rosie Carderelli summarized the message of the people of Mexico: "They are only one heartbeat away from heaven or hell. I got a burden for souls."

LYNCHBURG CHRISTIAN ACADEMY

At the opening bell at 8:20 each morning, approximately six hundred students have found their way into the modern two-story brick U-shaped complex which is the Lynchburg Christian Academy. Many ride the fifteen school buses from outlying areas around Lynchburg, while others are brought in car pools by parents. A few walk from the surrounding neighborhood.

As visitors walk the wide gleaming floors, definite impressions come through to them: the modern well-equipped rooms; the quiet, disciplined children moving through the halls; the respect for authority and rules; the obvious patriotism reflected in bulletin boards, posters, and the American flag. These impressions are reminiscent of the old-fashioned schools that made America great. Unlike the public school, the words of "Jesus Loves Me" and Scripture verses come from classroom doors, for the Academy is decidedly Christian in emphasis. A Bible lesson each day supplements the usual curriculum.

Kindergarten through grade twelve is offered at Lynchburg

Christian Academy, under the leadership of Vern Hammond, principal. The school was founded on high academic standards and, according to Sam Towns, student body president, he is learning more here than he did at the local high school last year.

Discipline is a forgotten word in education these days. The Academy believes in old-fashioned homework and that a student should learn some discipline as preparation for a productive life of service to the Lord and to his community. Discipline is reflected in skirt length on girls and hair length on fellows. As the younger classes move through the halls for recess or to chapel, the teachers maintain quiet. According to Dr. Jim Henry, chairman, Experimental School, Eastern Kentucky University, "I have never seen children so quiet in school in all my life."

Jerry Falwell began the Lynchburg Christian Academy in 1967 when he realized his three small children needed a Christian school to attend, then viewed the other parents in his congregation who needed a place to train their children in the Word of God and an old-fashioned preparation in academics. Falwell agreed with the staff members of the church that the current trend in experimentalism, including the philosophy of John Dewey, has eroded the morals of young people, softened the academic standards, and torn down allegiance to the United States.

Miss Libby Huff, music instructor in the high school, remarked, "The young people need to understand the nature of rock music and its effect on their lives." Miss Huff teaches students how to analyze music in relation to their own listening habits, the impact upon their moral lives, and the standards of Christianity.

3

THOMAS ROAD BAPTIST CHURCH IS PEOPLE

What is Thomas Road Baptist Church? It is more than bricks, pews, and windows. It is people! The Thomas Road Baptist Church is people, people whose lives have been transformed by the power of the gospel. The Thomas Road Baptist Church is people who have experienced the miraculous power of Calvary and in response live a supernatural Christian life for the glory of God.

Some churches are known for their elegant buildings. People travel long distances to take tours through their facilities. Some church buildings are known for their modern architectural achievements. Others are known for their nostalgic historical significance. A church may be remembered because of its unique steeple, an unusual altar, or the fact that famous people are buried there, such as Westminster Abbey, London, England. But a church is more than a building. People do not visit the Thomas Road Baptist Church to see the building; they come for other reasons.

What is Thomas Road Baptist Church? Some churches are known for their organization and administration. These churches hold conferences to teach others their organizational expertise. These churches spend energy on writing aims, job descriptions, and preparing role-of-authority charts. Committee meetings are frequent. Some pastors feel laymen should be involved in the local church, and the best involvement is sitting on committees (this is not practiced at Thomas Road Baptist Church). Such churches are

simply weekend country clubs, not New Testament churches. Ladies attend to show off their hairdos, and men find business contacts at such a typical American church. Thomas Road Baptist
Church is not built on organization nor is its ministry carried out by
constitutions and administration. Some visitors are even disappoint-
ed at the low priority given to organization at the Thomas Road
Baptist Church. Thomas Road is more than organization.

What is Thomas Road Baptist Church? Some churches are
known for their liturgy and worship services. Worshippers are
moved to reverent feelings by the deep tones of the organ, or by
seeing the pale sunlight filter through stained-glass windows. Printed
prayers, lighted candles, and formal singing are emphasized in these
church services. The Thomas Road Baptist Church does not emphasize a worship service. Men pray from the heart rather than
from printed prayers, people joyfully sing the gospel songs rather
than choir anthems and somber hymns. The service centers around
preaching the Bible and the invitation at the end of a sermon, when
people come to receive Jesus Christ. The Thomas Road Baptist
Church is more than worship. Worship is not a program, it's an attitude of the heart. According to Jerry Falwell, "We begin worship-
ping God when the first bus driver pulls on our lot to go out and
pick up children at 8:00 A.M. Sunday."

What is Thomas Road Baptist Church? The new movement today is to stress Koinonia fellowship groups. Some Christians retreat
to their living rooms for Bible study and fellowship. They say that
most churches have lost the gift of fellowship, so these churches
make fellowship their mandate. Dialogue becomes the purpose of
their existence. Such churches are small—by design. Such churches
do not invite the unsaved into their fellowship—by design. Such
churches are spiritually ingrown and sinfully selfish—by design. Although thousands attend Thomas Road Baptist Church, there is a
spirit of fellowship before and after the services. The sanctuary is
not considered sacred; people talk with their friends, chat with an

acquaintance, or sit reverently waiting for the service. Unbelievable as it may seem, there is fellowship among the multitude at Thomas Road Baptist Church. But Thomas Road is more than fellowship.

Thomas Road Baptist Church is *people*. Emphasis is not on buildings, organizations, worship, or other sidelines that characterize most American churches. People come by the thousands to the church. Over two thousand of them ride the Sunday-school buses. Junior-high school girls come in hot pants because they've never been taught differently and this might be their first time in the house of God. Some grade-school children come barefoot because they can't afford shoes and the Sunday-school bus drivers are so congenial that the children feel accepted, bare feet and all. Some people drive pickup trucks because they can't afford cars; others drive Cadillacs because they want to. The city bus line stops at the front door of the church—many come that way, paying the twenty-five-cent bus fare. A few who live in the neighborhood walk. It's much better that way because parking is so congested that many of those who drive have to park three or four blocks away from the church. Some who start out driving to Thomas Road Baptist Church don't make it. Parking has become so crowded and the lines of cars so long, that some visitors and members become discouraged, turn around, and go home. On Sundays when the policemen turn people away from the parking lots, some go to other churches.

Thomas Road Baptist Church is people. Some of the greatest in-depth conversions in America happen right in Thomas Road Baptist Church. Scores of convicts who have served time in jails and prisons now live good lives and attend the Thomas Road Baptist Church. At the same time there are millionaires and well-to-do businessmen who attend Thomas Road Baptist Church. Young boys raised in the church who have never tasted a sip of beer are in the Sunday school, while scores of men converted through Elim Home attend the church, some of them having gone to the bottom of the human ladder because of the sin of alcoholism. Social drink-

ers come to Thomas Road Baptist Church, even though Jerry Falwell preaches against liquor and the church as a whole opposes alcohol in any form. But the gospel makes them welcome and many
get saved. Young families attend Thomas Road Baptist Church because of its stand against worldly amusements. They want their
children reared in a church that will teach the Word of God. Also,
Thomas Road Baptist Church has shouting hillbillies who inter-
sperse the sermon with "Amen" or "Praise the Lord!" But all of
the members are not shouters; many worship God in their own reverent meditation, praising God inwardly for His wonderful words of
life. Teen-agers flock to Thomas Road Baptist Church and many of
them walk the aisles to find Jesus Christ as Saviour. When asked
why he attended, one high-school boy answered, "Thomas Road
Baptist Church is where the action is each weekend."

The Thomas Road Baptist Church is people. People serving,
people singing, people praying, people studying the Scriptures.
Churches that overemphasize buildings usually underemphasize
people. Churches that stress organization usually neglect people.
Churches that accentuate doctrine usually manipulate people.
Churches that glory in worship services usually repel people. The
Thomas Road Baptist Church has been successful because its ministry is *from* people *to* people. The church is a group of saved people who appreciate their salvation and want to reach other lost people with the gospel. The Thomas Road Baptist Church is a group of
saved people who place themselves under the discipline of the Word
of God so they may grow in the grace of God. Thomas Road Baptist Church is a group of people who feel that Jesus Christ is in their
church, compelling them to go into all the world and preach the
gospel to every creature. Because of that they baptize the lost, teach
the Word of God to children and adults, take collections to carry
out the work of the ministry, and construct buildings in which to
serve God. The Thomas Road Baptist Church is people.

Why do people come to Thomas Road Baptist Church? Who

knows? Some come seeking salvation from an enslaving habit, as a business executive who walked into Dr. Falwell's office asking for help with a drinking problem. He was afraid he was becoming an alcoholic. Some come seeking happiness, as a young wife who had tried dancing, extramarital sexual affairs, and drinking, but found nothing brought happiness. The first time she came, she walked the aisle and accepted Christ as her Saviour. Some come seeking forgiveness, as a young father who was guilty of pressuring his wife to get an abortion; he wondered if God would forgive him for murdering an unborn child. Some come seeking meaning in life, as a young college student who had found that sociology, psychology, and philosophy did not have the answer. He saw the peace in the young people of Thomas Road Baptist Church and wondered how they got it. Some come seeking a place to serve God, as a couple who came from a northern church; she had been in the Woman's Missionary Society and he had been on the decons' board, yet they wanted to become soul winners and reach lost people for Christ. The first time they attended the church they walked down the aisle and transferred their membership into Thomas Road Baptist Church.

The following are a few of the miracles at Thomas Road Baptist Church. These lives have been changed by the gospel and these people are now working and serving in some capacity at the Thomas Road Baptist Church. They give testimony to finding peace and contentment in their Christian service.

THE BROKEN HOME OF A GOSPEL SINGER

Jerry stood in the pulpit and jokingly said, "I want the biggest man in gospel music to come and sing for you." He laughed and the audience laughed with him, because of Doug Oldham's 315 pounds. Doug smiled as he picked up the microphone and walked to the edge of the steps to sing on "The Old-Time Gospel Hour," as he does each week. Last year he was voted the most popular Christian recording artist.

Doug dropped his head and told the audience that, even though he was reared in a Christian home, like many young people he had never had a personal relationship with Jesus Christ. After beginning college, he took a job as Minister of Music, though his music was not sung from the heart. Life became frustrating and confusing for Doug; the inconsistencies in his own life with the gospel songs he sang hardened his heart and made him difficult to get along with. As Doug stood before the masses at Thomas Road and looked into the television camera, he brushed a tear from his eye and indicated that he began attending places he shouldn't, and was sold out to the love of money. He treated his family terribly and his three small children, Paula, Karen, and Rebekah, were frightened and confused. Doug had been on national radio and television for another denomination, but at home his wife, Laura Lee, knew that he was a hypocrite. After nine years of pressure, tension and argument, she made her decision to leave Doug and try to evaluate the problems that filled their marriage.

When Laura Lee left Doug, he found himself with nothing. The home was lost, the big car was gone, and he ended up living in a small room in the back of a friend's house. One clear night as Doug drove in southern Ohio, the full impact of his problems crashed upon him. He prayed, "Lord, if you're up there, give me something worth living for." Doug points to this incident as the time he came to know Jesus Christ as Saviour from sin. His family was reunited and they have spent ten wonderful years together.

Shortly after the reunion, Doug took Rebekah and went to the old house to clean it up. After pushing a broom around the floors he realized Becky was missing. "Where are you?" he called. He found her in the living room between the front door and the wall, hiding. With frightened eyes, she looked up and said, "I don't like this house." The little girl could remember the years of beatings and fear.

That morning Doug stood on the platform of the Thomas Road
Baptist Church, pushed his head back, and with unashamed tears
sang "Thanks to Calvary I Don't Live Here Anymore."

Today I went back to the place where I used to go,
Today I saw the same old crowd I knew before.
When they asked me what had happened, I tried to tell them,
"Thanks to Calvary I don't come here anymore."

Thanks to Calvary I am not the man I used to be;
Thanks to Calvary things are different than before.
While the tears ran down my face, I tried to tell them,
"Thanks to Calvary I don't come here anymore."

And then we went back to the house where we used to live;
My little girl ran and hid behind the door.
I said, "Honey, never fear. You've got a new daddy—
Thanks to Calvary we don't live here anymore."

Thanks to Calvary, I am not the dad I used to be.
Thanks to Calvary, things are different than before.
While the tears ran down my face, I tried to tell her,
"Thanks to Calvary we don't live here anymore."

"Dad could always sing," his eldest daughter, Paula, commented,
"but it wasn't until ten years ago that he found out what singing was
all about."

The younger girl, Rebekah, often chimes in with a hearty "He's
really changed—he's a terrific dad." The middle daughter, Karen,
adds, "He's changed all right, but he couldn't do it in himself—it
was Jesus."

Often Doug will bring the family to the platform to sing with
him. One of the favorites at the Thomas Road Baptist Church is
"Heaven Came Down and Glory Filled My Soul."

Laura adds a final convincing testimony to the change in Doug's life: "He's a great singer—but he's a better husband and father."

A SIXTY-FOUR-TIME LOSER FINALLY WINS

Red Witt had sixty-four convictions and served time in the Richmond State Penitentiary, as well as being in and out of the Lynchburg Jail and others in surrouning counties. He served time for stealing, drinking, gambling, and fighting, and he bears in his body the scars of sin. He was shot on two different occasions and another time was peppered with shotgun pellets on the back of his neck and head. He was knifed with five inches of coal steel and, according to his testimony, "I used to wonder why God let me live." In prison, he read the Bible through several times. Red came from a Christian home and, when his dad died, he knew the only way he was going to see him again was to get saved. From his boyhood he knew the plan of salvation, but he had never made the decision to accept Jesus Christ. The older he grew, the deeper he spiraled into sin. Red was involved in the numbers racket and ran bootleg liquor in the trunk in his automobile.

Sandra, his wife, knew the status of their life and asked Red to attend church with her. It was a Southern Baptist church with no evangelistic outreach, but it did preach the gospel. There, Red accepted Christ as his Saviour, but the hypocrisy of some members confused Sandra. She had felt that Christians should live their faith. What she saw on the inside of the church was no different than the world outside. A friend came to Red and gave him advice that changed his whole life. The friend pointed out that his past prison record and life of sin was not acceptable to the sophisticated church they were attending. Red went a few blocks away to the Thomas Road Baptist Church. The first time he attended there was such a crowd that he had to sit on the floor. Red knew that any church that attracted the masses of people and had such enthusiastic preaching must be in the center of God's will. He recognized Thomas Road members from the wrong side of the law. These had been saved at Thomas Road Baptist Church. He went forward that night, giving his entire life to Jesus Christ.

Even though Sandra had suggested that Red go to church, she became rebellious and resentful at the change in him. At the time she was under the care of a psychiatrist. Red began witnessing to his wife, asking her to become a Christian. The past had been cruel and she rationalized that he was pretending to be a Christian to keep her from divorcing him. Because she misread his motives, she left him.

Red asked the faithful prayer group at Thomas Road Baptist Church to pray for Sandra's salvation, and they did. The couple's separation lasted about a year. Red visited her regularly and prayed for her. Each time they talked, he witnessed to her about his changed life in Jesus Christ. He promised her that if she would come home, life would be different for the two of them. Sandra could not get over the love she had for Red and hesitantly came home.

Red faithfully attended the Thomas Road Baptist Church and invited his wife to go with him. She refused, saying she wanted no part of religion and the fanatics at Thomas Road. Sometimes she'd curse him for even asking her. He would go to church alone and not try to force her. Sandra would stay home alone and think, "He really is different." There was a time that he'd never let her say such things to him. Sandra decided that, since he was trying so hard, she'd go with him. For a few months she sat under the gospel at Thomas Road Baptist Church. On Homecoming Day, 1967, she accepted Christ as personal Saviour. Life was different. Sandra went one last time to the psychiatrist. The doctor said, "You and I don't have anything to talk about anymore."

Red and Sandra began serving Christ together. They prayed about the right place of service and put their complete faith in the God of their salvation.

Jerry Falwell mentioned that a man was coming from the Bill

Rice Ranch in Murfreesboro, Tennessee, to teach the sign language
to all who desired to learn. Red and Sandra prayed about this and
attended the two-week college-level seminar, learning the deaf language. Sandra's deaf friend in the factory where she worked was the
first to benefit from the program. The Witts' teacher, Don Cabbage,
led the deaf woman to Christ. This impressed Sandra with the need
for telling the deaf about Jesus. She learned that 800 deaf people
die every day, and 740 of them never even heard of Christ.

Although Lynchburg has only a small deaf community, the first
and most faithful to come was Mrs. Perry, Sandra's friend from the
factory. There are now eleven who come, but many more are saved
in meetings and special services. Red Witt faithfully brings, for every service, the deaf who have no other way to come.

A TEEN-AGER FINDS CHRIST—LATER HE
BUILDS A CHURCH

The Thomas Road Baptist Church has held many revivals since
its beginning in 1956, and no man can rightly judge which was the
most successful. The Freddie Gage Youth Crusade in February,
1972, witnessed over fourteen hundred decisions for Jesus Christ.
The Jack Van Impe Crusade in November, 1970, recorded over
eight hundred decisions for Christ, and so it goes. Every revival has
resulted directly or indirectly in drunkards saved from the curse of
alcohol, prostitutes saved from their beds of sin, and families united
through Christ. But perhaps the greatest joy comes when a soul is
gloriously saved and surrenders for full-time Christian service, to
preach the gospel and go to his Jerusalem to build another superaggressive church such as Jerry Falwell has done in Lynchburg. One
of these was Rudy Holland.

Eternity will reveal how many were influenced as a result of
Brother Lester Roloff's revival at Thomas Road, March 28 to
April 3, 1965. On April 1, Rudy W. Holland attended for the first

time. At eighteen, young Holland had yet to accept Christ as his Saviour. Since the previous Saturday night, his rebellious attitude toward God and the church had softened.

With three friends, Rudy had gone to a dance in Bedford, twenty-five miles from Lynchburg, on that Saturday, March 27. All four had been drinking heavily, and with their bottled courage had decided to crash the dance, even though they had been warned to stay away. Several Bedford area boys decided to teach the intruders a lesson and were converging on the unwelcome quartet with knives and chains when the Bedford police arrived to stop what might have been a murder. Young Holland and his friends were escorted back to Lynchburg by the Virginia State Police.

The haunting thought of death had lingered in Rudy's mind since that night and with the relentless pressure from his parents to attend the services, he had come. He had even sat with his parents, something he had not done for months. As the congregation stood to sing the hymn of invitation, Rudy Holland's muscles tensed. His heart beat faster and louder as Brother Roloff pleaded for the unsaved to step out for Jesus. The palms of his hands became wet with perspiration and his knuckles turned white as he fiercely gripped the back of the pew in front of him.

As Lester Roloff began to sing "Harvest Time," every word pierced young Holland's heart. Tears streamed from his eyes. He wanted to step out, he knew he needed to receive Christ as his Saviour, but he held back.

"I'll go with you, son!" said his mother; she pressed her hand on her son's tightly clenched fist. Rudy stepped out at once and walked down the aisle of Thomas Road Baptist Church to the altar, where he was met by an elderly white-haired gentleman named Mr. Mayberry (at eighty years of age still an active member today) who showed him God's simple plan of salvation. Rudy left the services a new creature, professing his faith in Jesus Christ.

Graduation from high school came two months later and in September, 1965, Rudy enrolled at Tennessee Temple College, Chattanooga, Tennessee. In 1967 he surrendered to God's call to preach. After much prayer, he decided to start a church in Roanoke, Virginia, after he received his degree.

"We're a new church with an old message about a living Saviour!" states Holland enthusiastically. At twenty-five years of age, the young preacher has accomplished much in reaching the Roanoke-Salem area for Christ. His new church, the Berean Baptist Church, began on July 12, 1970, with a family of four. Two years later, the church averaged 325 in Sunday school. The church's fifteen-minute radio program, "Moments of Inspiration," is heard five days a week by a large audience in the area. Holland has started six Sunday-school bus routes, the church owns ten acres of prime land on an expressway where a new $70,000, 400-seat auditorium has been built, and plans are now being made to immediately expand the already overcrowded Sunday-school wing. Falwell considers Rudy Holland a son in the ministry. What Holland has done in Roanoke, Falwell believes can be done all over America by the thousands of Lynchburg Baptist College students who will go out to start superaggressive local churches.

SATURATION EVANGELISM REACHES A SUCCESSFUL BUSINESSMAN

Wayne Booth, successful contractor and businessman, found Christ at Thomas Road Baptist Church through an application of saturation evangelism and the outreach of Elim Home. Wayne's father was taken to Elim Home in 1968 with what was called an incurable drinking problem. A couple of days later, the elderly Booth called his son and asked for a Bible—a small request, thought the son. After Gordon Booth left Elim Home, Wayne noticed a change in his life and a love for Thomas Road Baptist Church. His father attended every Sunday and tried to get him to attend. The first time

Wayne came to Thomas Road was the result of a contest; his father was trying to win a Scofield Bible by getting ten guests in Sunday school. Wayne had never seen Thomas Road Baptist Church, even though he had contributed bricks to build a workshop at Elim Home, constructed by his father. That Sunday morning, the elderly Booth had brought thirty-nine to Sunday school and got a special set of Christian books. After that, the father phoned Wayne on Sundays, inviting him to church.

The elderly Booth died in December, 1969. Falwell preached the funeral sermon and talked to Wayne about salvation. During this time alcohol was having an increasing influence on Wayne and he spent time drinking with the fellows on the job, rather than at home. Domestic problems were plaguing the Booths, and their marriage was on the verge of divorce. Helen Booth called Falwell asking for help, and that he might talk with Wayne. After that Jerry sent Wayne postcards inviting him to church nearly every time he went out of town. Weekly, Falwell had his secretary phone Booth's office. Conditions in the home grew steadily worse. Wayne attended church but did not respond to the invitation. His wife filed for divorce and there seemed no solution but to dissolve the marriage. One more postcard came and, as a result, Wayne Booth visited the church on Wednesday evening, March 3, 1971. During the invitation he went forward and received Christ as Saviour. Helen had already been saved. Their home was put back together.

Wayne Booth has become a witness for Christ among businessmen throughout the southeast, as his business stretches from Maryland to South Carolina. Falwell has taken advantage of his business ability, placing him as an advisor on the church financial committee. Many times when the church plane is not available, Booth flies Falwell or Towns to preaching appointments in his Cessna 310. Also, he pilots the church plane, a Cessna 414. He and two other businessmen, Joe Leonard and Bill Burruss, made the Cessna 414 available to the church for the outreach of evangelism. Booth's conversion is a testimony to the principle of saturation evangelism: reaching every available person by every available means at every available time.

A YOUNG HUSBAND FINDS PURPOSE IN LIFE

"Why don't you go and hear Jerry Falwell preach?" Harry Dean's mother-in law asked him.

The troubled young man didn't really think that would do any good. He had heard little about Jerry Falwell, except that he had a big church, and he had seen his picture on a billboard along Route 460 just outside of Lynchburg. Life wasn't what Harry wanted it to be. There was problem after problem to contend with. Worldly influences had been gnawing at his marriage ties. The family seemed headed for trouble, but Harry didn't know what to do about it.

It was not only his marriage he worried about. What about his career? The unsettled future plagued him continuously. Harry had spent four years at Virginia Polytechnical Institute in Blacksburg, Virginia, hoping to prepare himself for something—but what?

At Virginia Tech he met his wife, Margaret, and married her while still a student. Harry became discouraged and dropped out of college. The couple moved to Roanoke, where he got a job as a pharmaceutical salesman. It was just a job and had nothing to do with his ambitions.

They became members of a small Presbyterian Church in Roanoke. Seeking spiritual fulfillment, Harry decided to apply at Union Theological Seminary in Richmond—in his mind, a great step toward helping mankind. The liberal Presbyterian church had paved the way for this humanitarian decision. Harry was searching desperately for meaning, success, and happiness in life. Remembering the suggestion of his mother-in-law to go hear Jerry Falwell preach, Harry decided to visit Thomas Road. One day, on his regular sales trip to Lynchburg, he stopped in. He was met by Jim Soward (former associate pastor of Thomas Road Baptist Church) who took him on a tour of the premises. He was fortunate enough to meet Jerry personally and talk with him. "We're having a television rally in Roanoke. Why don't you come?" Jerry asked. Harry promised to do so.

Harry doesn't remember a word Jerry said that night at the rally. "It was the invitation that got me," he said. "My wife and I both went forward. Rudy Holland, a young pastor saved under Jerry's ministry, led us to the Lord."

That night, while they talked with Jerry, he warned them of the danger of a liberal church. He counseled them to join a Bible-believing, Bible-preaching church. They meant business and heeded Jerry's advice. They joined Rudy Holland's church in Roanoke, where they received good Bible teaching.

Today, Harry is a student at Lynchburg Baptist College, training for full-time Christian service. If you were to visit the Deans' home today, you would find it warm and happy. Harry affirms, "I don't know what the future holds for me. One thing I know—it's bright!"

A TRUCK DRIVER FINDS CHRIST

How many times does God have to knock a man down before he listens to Him? Malon Jones, a transfer truck driver, lived across the street from Thomas Road Baptist Church. Four years ago on a Sunday evening while driving under the influence of alcohol, Jones was stopped by a policeman for weaving all over the road. The policeman gave Mr. Jones a ticket and took his car to the station. Because Malon had previously been picked up for drunken driving, this time he felt the judge would send him to jail; he would lose his license and his job.

His oldest daughter, Mrs. Nancy McGuire, who had been saved at Thomas Road Baptist Church, lived just down the street. When he got home Malon went to see her, knowing what she would say:

"The accidents are God's warnings." Malon didn't want to hear about God, so he didn't stay. He asked his daughter Brenda to take him to get his car. When Malon began weeping and started praying, she was sure he was losing his mind. "God," he cried, "help me and I'll never touch another drop of alcohol."

The next week was hard for Malon Jones. He quit being his loud, boisterous self. The following Sunday morning he got up and informed the family, "I am going to church." No one in the family could believe it. "I had never seen my father go to church in my life," Nancy said afterward; "I was shocked." "I hadn't been to church for twenty or thirty years," Malon remembers. "The family attended that Sunday-morning service at Thomas Road. I don't know why it was Thomas Road—probably because it was closest," he said. Malon had previously held nothing but contempt for Jerry Falwell and had been vocal about it.

That Sunday night he went back to church and during the invitation he walked down the aisle and accepted Christ as his Saviour. Since that night in 1968, he has stopped drinking and has lived a happy life. Malon has become one of Jerry Falwell's greatest supporters. "There's nobody like Jerry," he testifies. "And do you know, I never knew I had a family until I got saved!"

A DRIFTER LANDS ON THE ROCK

James M. Wright has been called Shorty all his life; even in full manhood he is only five feet, four inches tall. He was a slave to alcohol; drink destroyed his life and his family. Shorty came from a Christian family in West Virginia and started drinking on weekends in his early twenties. When he got away from the influence of the Christian home, he began getting drunk every night. He was married in 1940 and had one child, but his wife left him eleven years later. Shorty began traveling from one job to another—he was a short-order cook, worked on an assembly line, was a laborer in a rock quarry, and a stevedore in a warehouse. He confessed, "I had no friends and drifted from flophouse to flophouse. Many nights I had no bed and slept out under the trees in the park or in the woods. I just lay down and went to sleep wherever the night would catch me." His life was an endless succession of getting jobs and losing them because of drinking. He drifted from Massachusetts to Florida and even lived on the famed New York Bowery.

Shorty came to Lynchburg in 1959 to stay with his brother, and after two months, he confesses, "He couldn't put up with my drinking any longer." Bill Lawhorne told Shorty about Elim Home. He went sober but thirsting after drink. He attended the Bible study conducted each day, as was required, and tried reading his Bible, but he couldn't understand the Scriptures. He prayed many times a day, but now as Shorty looks back he realizes, "God couldn't hear me because I didn't pray the sinner's prayer— 'God be merciful to me a sinner.' " After a couple of weeks he received Jesus Christ and testified, "I got my life straightened out and found that what I had been searching for all the time was the sweet peace that comes by turning everything over to God."

Shorty is an usher and deacon at the Thomas Road Baptist Church. He has not touched a drop of alcohol since his conversion thirteen years ago. While at Elim Home, Mae Turner and other ladies came from Appomattox, Virginia, to provide transportation for the men of Elim Home to Thomas Road Baptist Church. Shorty became acquainted with Mae and married her after he left Elim. Today they serve God together and Shorty praises his Saviour for the new life he has in Jesus Christ.

A FATHER FINDS FAITH

Red Rhodenhizer sat in the living room of his house, a broken man, recognizing that alcohol had become the master of his life. The bottle had come between him and his family and now his job was in jeopardy. Red sat thinking about the life of a co-worker. That man's life was different; he prayed before opening his lunch pail. He had once told Red that he should try life with Christ.

In tears, Red at last phoned this Christian man for help. Within the hour, that friend and two other Christian laymen visited his home, giving the gospel to Red and his wife. On their knees by the living-room couch, Red and Frances Rhodenhizer accepted Christ as their personal Saviour.

Red testifies, "God took the thirst for alcohol away immediately." But other sins in his life bothered him. Red started attending Thomas Road Baptist Church and hearing God's Word preached. "I soon learned that it was through Bible study and prayer that a Christian grew strong."

When Thomas Road Baptist Church decided to expand its bus ministry, Pastor Falwell gave Red the first new bus route. For the first time in his life Red had a responsibility where others depended upon him for help. "I look back now and thank Jerry for his faith in me. I needed the responsibility for the souls of those children." Over the years since then Red has been among the most faithful, missing only three Sundays in all the years. He is a pastor to all who ride his bus.

Red had been very close to his own two boys and had always tried to have them in church on Sunday morning. The boys, then twelve and fourteen years old, attended a local church which did not preach salvation. They saw the change in their parent's life and soon the whole family attended Thomas Road Baptist Church. Red's son David, now studying for the ministry at Lynchburg Baptist College, states, "It wasn't long before my brother and I were saved and serving the Lord." Dave has also participated in Thomas Road Baptist Church's bus ministry.

Red tells the story of one small boy who always gave him trouble on the bus. He once broke all the overhead lights on the bus. With love and patience through the years, Red saw this young man grow up, accept Christ, and last fall enroll in Lynchburg Baptist College, to prepare himself for reaching still others.

BACKSLIDDEN FOR TEN YEARS

During the early sixties, Rick Sanders, a junior-high-school student, spent a few days with his aunt and uncle, Mr. and Mrs. Bill Greene, and attended the Thomas Road Baptist Church. As he heard Jerry Falwell preach, God spoke to his heart. Rich went forward with his twin brother and accepted Jesus Christ as Saviour. He returned to a nearby town, was baptized, and joined a local church. Sanders testifies that he never had victory over sin for the next ten years because he lacked proper encouragement and instruction in the Christian life. Soon he forgot about that night in 1961 when he accepted Jesus Christ.

After graduation from high school, he entered the army and according to his testimony, "Then was when my real troubles started —nothing went right." Sanders began drinking and partying on the weekends. His life seemed to be one long drudgery from morning to evening. When he became tired of beer and pointless living, he went to the base chaplain for counseling, yet this did not help him. He continued in his sinful ways. Next, a painful kidney infection sent him to the hospital, where his despondency grew. He visited a psychiatrist, who thought Sanders would be happier out of the army; within a few weeks he had an honorable discharge.

Sanders returned to Lynchburg and secured a job as the manager of a department store. With each new raise in pay came a progressive round of drinking and parties. Sanders testified that he drank from 5:00 P.M. to midnight on the weekends to find escape from reality.

During this time he received a shock—his older sister committed suicide on the same day that his father had done so eight years before, February 29. Two years later a girl not even known to Sanders almost died on his living-room floor. As a friend gave her artificial respiration, Sanders called on God. He was frightened because drugs were the suspected cause of her sudden collapse and he was afraid of going to jail because she was underage. Sanders promised God that if the girl lived, he would serve Him. Even though the prayer was selfish, he meant what he said. In the early hours of the morning, the girl stood up and left the apartment with her friend. Sanders forgot his promise, even though God did not.

A short time later, his roommate came in while Rick was drinking and asked him to go to church. According to Sanders, "The idea strangely appealed to me and I decided that I would go." Two Sunday-school teachers from Jordan Baptist Church, Lynchburg, came and witnessed to him and he began to remember the things that had happened to him ten years before. Sanders rededicated his life to the Lord that night. Even though he quit drinking immediately, smoking lingered as a habit. As Sanders spent time in the Word of God and church attendance, God delivered him from his habit.

One day at work, God dealt with Sanders. According to him, "I didn't know what it was God wanted, so I picked up my Bible and began to read. The next thing I knew I was telling the Lord that I would do anything He wanted me to do and go anywhere He wanted me to go. It was clear in my heart and mind that He wanted me to leave my job. I quit right then. I lived a mountaintop experience for many weeks after that. I lost all desire for earthly things and sold most of my household goods to pay my bills. God was preparing me to become a student at Lynchburg Baptist College." Sanders finally testifies, "What I said that day at work remains my life's ambition—to do anything God wants."

A DRUNK SOBERS UP

E. K. White quit school at seventeen, left home, and had rambling on his mind, traveling throughout Virginia. He testified, "I was a smart know-it-all." He felt that pretty girls, honky-tonks, and whiskey were the path to happiness. For a while he thought he could handle whiskey, then it began to handle him. E. K. White went from job to job in Richmond, Virginia, and Washington, D.C., searching for something, but not knowing what he was seeking. He decided to return home and see his mother. He was involved in a grinding car accident; although he was not hurt, the man driving the car died. He testified, "That is when I began to seek God; I knew He must have been in the car protecting me." White continued drinking, although his thoughts were on God. His mother worried; his brother and ex-state trooper Bill Kaufman (now on the staff of the church) came to witness to them about the Lord Jesus Christ. Later Bill Kaufman came to Mr. White's trailer and told him about Elim Home and Mr. Ray Horsley, its superintendent. At Elim Home, E. K. received Christ and testifies, "I can't explain everything God and Elim Home did for me but I have been sober for a number of years." White went on to testify, "Elim Home is not a place where you are locked up but a home for drunks where they teach you about the Lord who can change your life." White adds that God took everything from him so he would go to Elim Home and see the light of salvation. Now he testifies that God has given everything back to him and more.

A COLLEGE STUDENT FINDS JESUS CHRIST

Gene Albert began seeking God in his late teens when he was attending a Lutheran church and was sprinkled with holy water. He sought satisfaction through avenues which thousands of misguided young people seek to attain today. Gene was a good-looking basketball player when he graduated from Clear Spring High School, Clear Spring, Maryland, in 1970, as president of the senior class and holder of various sports awards.

In the fall of that year, Gene entered a four-year liberal arts college in western Maryland, majoring in psychology, hoping to go on from this major to become a Lutheran minister. He was in college only a couple of months when he found his whole life revolving around getting, selling, and using different kinds of drugs. His grades were fair the first semester, but as the second semester rolled around, the drugs started to show up on college papers and in his overall attitude. Gene testifies, "By this time my hair was shoulder length and everyone in my hometown knew I was taking drugs, including the police."

In the summer of 1971, Gene decided he couldn't go back to the same college because within his heart he knew there had to be something more to life. He started searching for a college in which to enroll. Practically the whole summer slipped by and still he had found no place to go to school. In the middle of August, Gene decided he wanted to go to Bible school and become a minister. He states, "I knew my Lutheran church didn't preach the Bible, so I went to Reverend Bill Freed, a fundamentalist minister I had heard a couple of years before at a little country church while preaching a revival. (I don't know what I, a Lutheran, was doing at a revival!) When I walked into his office with my long hair, blue jeans, and sneakers, I'll never forget the look Reverend Freed gave me." The pastor asked Gene what he wanted. "I told him I was looking for a Bible college to attend." Reverend Freed said all the Bible schools he knew required a student to be born again. Gene testifies, "So I lied to him and told him that I was born again." Gene figured the minister must have thought he was saved and just not separated, as are a lot of Christians. On his desk was a copy of the *Sword of the Lord* with ads about Bible colleges. He looked it over and recommended Tennessee Temple and Lynchburg Baptist College. For some reason, as soon as Gene saw the ad for Lynchburg Baptist College he knew he had to attend that school.

Immediately after he got home from Pastor Bill Freed's office, Gene called Dr. Elmer Towns, vice-president of Lynchburg Baptist College, and arranged for an interview. Gene thought about getting a wig and putting it over his long hair, because he knew if Reverend

Freed disapproved of it, Dr. Towns would also disapprove. Since he didn't want anything to stop him from getting accepted at Lynchburg Baptist College, he got his hair cut the day before the interview.

Gene saw Dr. Towns at about 11:30 A.M. The interview went smoothly, even when Towns asked about his conversion; by this time Gene was ready with a bigger and better conversion (lie) than the last one. At the end of the interview, Dr. Towns asked if there was anything else that he should know. Today Gene asks, "Do you think he asked me that because I had a pack of cigarettes in my shirt pocket?" He confesses, "I didn't know any better; I thought most Christians smoked. At least they did at my Lutheran church, and the pastor never said anything about it." Gene was given tentative acceptance that same day, and felt it was worth getting his hair cut. He states, "I felt I just had to get accepted."

When Lynchburg Baptist College opened its doors several weeks later, Gene was there. Dr. Towns and Dr. Falwell taught a class on the Introduction to Christian Life. For the first time since Gene could remember, he heard preaching on separation from the world, and since he was still part of the world, and not saved, conviction began to eat at his heart. Pretty soon he found himself lying awake in the early morning hours with deep conviction in his soul. He had always had too much pride to go forward at the invitation. On September 29, 1971, Gene couldn't fight the conviction any longer. He now reflects, "I knew what I had to do and as soon as I took the first step out of the pew, my burdens seemed to roll away and I could tell that the Lord saved me. I could see for the first time that what I was searching for in the Lutheran church, drugs, and all those other things could be found only in Jesus Christ, my new Lord and Saviour."

Since that time, Gene has seen his brother, sister, and his best friend and his wife, and many other lost loved ones come to the saving knowledge of Jesus Christ.

Now Gene Albert drives a Sunday-school bus to Roanoke every

Sunday and has had as many as sixty riders. Also, Gene is a back-up cameraman on number 4 in the small TV studio. His life is filled with purpose and satisfaction as he serves Jesus Christ.

A CHURCH MEMBER—BUT LOST

Mary Cox was raised in a Christian church, and was baptized when she was seven years old. After her marriage, she joined a Methodist church and raised her four children in a Methodist Sunday school. In 1966, she was working as a cashier in a grocery store with Peggy Arthur, a member of the Thomas Road Baptist Church. Peggy asked her to come to "Friend Day" at Thomas Road Baptist Church and help her win a Bible. According to Mary, "She kept after me to go with her, but I told her I went to church every Sunday. Since she persisted, I finally told her I would go but she would have to come by and pick up me and my son because I did not drive."

When Mary first attended Thomas Road, she testified, "I could feel the presence of God when I walked into the church. I had never seen so many Bibles; in our Methodist church we had always studied from literature." After that, Mary got a small Bible and began studying the Scriptures. Each Sunday her friend would come by and drive her to Sunday school. On July 16, 1966, Mary Cox went forward and received Jesus Christ as her personal Saviour. She had read in her Bible, "Behold, I stand at the door, and knock: if any man hear my voice, and open the door, I will come in" (Revelation 3:20). Mary testified that she knew Christ was knocking at her heart's door and she received Him as Saviour. Immediately after salvation she claimed the promise, "Believe on the Lord Jesus Christ, and thou shalt be saved, and thy house" (Acts 16:31). She claimed that promise, and through prayer and faith her whole family has come to know Jesus Christ—husband, son, daughter, and daughter-in-law. Mary has taught six-year-old girls for the past five years in Sunday school and testifies, "These have been the happiest years of our married life. Thank God for a Sunday-school contest and a friend who cared to invite me to church."

TESTIMONY OF A CHRISTIAN FROM ANOTHER CHURCH IN LYNCHBURG, VIRGINIA

Billy Price, a six-foot, twenty-year-old Christian worker, lives in Lynchburg, home of the fastest-growing church in America (Thomas Road Baptist Church), yet he does not attend Thomas Road. Jordan Baptist Church, a small church with a small attendance, is his place for serving God.

How does living in the shadow of a large church affect Billy's life and his church? "The effect is tremendous! How can it be anything else? When I visit for my church in one out of every two homes they usually ask if I am from Thomas Road. Lynchburg has been so well saturated that there is not a home in the immediate area which does not know the name Jerry Falwell and, in turn, what it stands for." Price went on to comment, "I personally benefit, and I am sure other local churches benefit from the excellent Bible speakers and evangelists brought in through Thomas Road."

The example of Thomas Road Baptist Church is always before the other churches as a visual demonstration of what God can do through a local church. Through the ministries of Thomas Road, many hidden blessings shower on the neighborhood churches. Many unsaved people in Lynchburg are familiar with the gospel because of the television and radio outreach of Thomas Road Baptist Church.

The practical helps provided by Thomas Road are numerous and effective. Billy's church is an example. "We had never operated a bus route until Thomas Road Baptist Church had experienced great success with theirs. Also, the success of Thomas Road Baptist Church with Christian education inspired my church to undertake a Christian day nursery," Billy stated. He indicated other areas of help. "Thomas Road has a pastors' conference every summer, and recently a youth and bus conference were held. These provide several days of intensive training for Christian workers at my church."

Speaking as a student of Lynchburg Baptist College, Price added, "One of the most effective innovations of Thomas Road Baptist Church in recent years is Lynchburg Baptist College. I feel that this college provides excellent training for pastors and laymen who wish to equip themselves for God's service. The real impact of this college will not be felt for years, but it will be tremendous."

Billy was asked if there were any bad effects of Thomas Road Baptist Church. "No, not really. There will always be jealousy among pastors and churches, but I definitely believe the ill effects are minimal, compared to the good effects."

Thomas Road Baptist Church has been inspirational to Billy. "When I become discouraged in my spiritual efforts, I can ride down Thomas Road and see the magnificent undertaking and realize that God blesses faithful service. One Sunday morning on my way to my own church, I was thrilled to see nine huge yellow Thomas Road Baptist Church buses on the expressway at once, packed to the brim with laughing children on their way to church."

Billy describes Thomas Road's affect on him personally: "I now attend Lynchburg Baptist College, my greatest personal contact with Thomas Road Baptist Church. I see how the TV, radio, and printed ministry affects every Christian life, and it aids me in my own Christian experience. There is a definite benefit in our city for the gospel of Christ. The church's effects are so far-reaching it is hard to narrow the results to one area or one person, but I believe the church's reputation in Lynchburg speaks for itself. I honestly doubt that there is one person in Lynchburg, who has lived here any length of time, who has never heard of Thomas Road or Jerry Falwell. If you ask about the church, most people will reply, 'It's a group of people concerned about being saved.' This is what I call a *testimony*."

4

WHAT IS A GREAT CHURCH?

Many observers have stated that the greatest church since Pentecost can be built at Thomas Road. This speculation was increased with the recent announcement by Dr. Falwell of a two-hundred-acre property acquisition and a moving of the church. The prospects for the future are limitless. "We plan to move from our 3,180-seat auditorium and build a 10,000-seat auditorium." According to a Christian magazine editor in Wheaton, Illinois, the new church building will be the largest church building in the history of Christianity.

Not only will the building be large, but the ministry will be worldwide and all-inclusive of the total needs of man. Dr. Falwell speaks of retirement homes, orphanages, and expansion of the college, in addition to the already productive alcoholic ministry, prison ministry, and camp ministry. Couple this outreach with the fact that the gospel reaches from Thomas Road into thousands of homes through the miracle of television and add the ministry of radio, heard over approximately one hundred stations daily. Dr. Falwell preaches to more people in one Sunday's services than the Apostle Paul did in his lifetime.

If we state that Thomas Road Baptist Church *can* be the greatest church since Pentecost, the natural question follows: What constitutes *greatness* in a local church? Greatness is not measured by size only, though attendance must be counted in greatness, along with finances, Bible teaching, outreach, spiritual power, dedication of service, and quality of life of those who attend the church.

Sociologists have used the following points to measure church greatness: (1) numerical growth, (2) involvement of members in the total ministry, and (3) the change in those who attend the church. These three points, along with two other biblical reasons, will measure a great church: (4) ministering to the total needs of members, and (5) saturation evangelism. These last two points have been neglected by most churches since Pentecost. The Thomas Road Baptist Church meets the qualifications of these five points; therefore, it could be called one of the greatest churches since Pentecost.

GREAT CHURCHES WIN MANY PEOPLE TO CHRIST AND GROW IN NUMBER

First, greatness involves numerical growth. Dr. W. A. Criswell, First Baptist Church, Dallas, Texas, stated, "There is nothing wrong with a small church, but there is something wrong with a church that is not growing." The Thomas Road Baptist Church is growing and attempting to fulfill the Great Commission by going into all of the world and making disciples. When sinners hear the gospel, then believe in Jesus Christ and follow Him, they become a part of a local church. All those who become a part of a local church can be counted, whether we number attendance or membership.

We live in a day when many people criticize numerical growth. However, emphasis on numbers is scriptural. The fourth book in the Bible is called Numbers; Jesus had disciples and they numbered twelve, 120 persons gathered in the Upper Room. On the Day of Pentecost 3,000 were added to the church and later 5,000 more. The reason God emphasizes numbers in Scripture is to prove that His church is growing and making numerical gains. We believe that quantity growth is reflective of quality growth.

The growth of the Thomas Road Baptist Church in the past few years is perhaps unparalleled in history. Sixteen years ago thirty-five adults gathered in a bankrupt bottling plant to begin the Thomas Road Baptist Church. In the past six years attendance has spiralled upward:

1967—1250
1968—2618
1969—2640
1970—3386
1971—4857
1972—5622

Last spring attendance jumped approximately fifteen hundred per week over last year, primarily due to the spring campaign, the Twelve Disciples. Each week a lesson on one of the disciples was taught, and those who came faithfully received a charm likeness of that disciple along with a picture.

In a day when mainline denominations are declining in attendance and financial income, the Thomas Road Baptist Church continues to grow. But numbers alone are not important. Numbers reflect the lost who are saved, then baptized, and finally attend Sunday school and church faithfully to study the Word of God.

The Great Commission is the marching orders of Thomas Road Baptist Church. "Go ye therefore, and teach all nations, baptizing them in the name of the Father, and of the Son, and of the Holy Ghost: Teaching them to observe all things whatsoever I have commanded you" (Matthew 28:19,20). The Great Commission has a three-fold sequence. First, get people saved, second, get people baptized, and third, get people to study the Bible. According to Falwell, "I find this formula simple to follow; it's what we do at Thomas Road Baptist Church, getting people saved, baptized, and attending Sunday school where the Bible is taught. Also, I am appalled that so many churches miss God's formula and spin off on tangents. Churches that stick to the Great Commission will grow—we'll do that."

Last year many received Christ and 510 were baptized. The continued evangelistic outreach, week after week for the past sixteen years, qualified Thomas Road Baptist Church as a great church. Sixteen years is not long when measured by almost two millenniums since Christ. There have been many great revivals and large crowds gathered in the name of Christ. But Thomas Road Baptist Church is a local church that is gathered each week and reflects growth each week. In our modern day of instant breakfast and instant neighborhood, the sixteen-year growth of Thomas Road Baptist Church stands as a miracle that God is still building great churches.

GREAT CHURCHES GET MEMBERS INVOLVED

Greatness is measured by the involvement of people in the ministry of the church. The Thomas Road Baptist Church is people carrying out the Great Commission and attempting to fulfill the Scripture in their lives. Dr. Falwell does not measure involvement as most American preachers do, that is, by committee attendance. Whereas the typical American church is structured by committees such as Woman's Missionary Society, Men's Brotherhood, education committees, and stewardship committees, the Thomas Road Baptist Church has only one functioning committee: the deacons. Falwell believes that his people should be involved in the ministry of the church, witnessing and working to reach their community. "Sitting on committees does not involve a person in the ministry nor does it edify the person," according to Falwell. Over one hundred people work in the Sunday-school bus ministry. Another large multitude of workers are involved in teaching the Sunday school. And Falwell asked the question, "Have you ever thought about how many ushers it takes to park cars, seat people, take up collections, and supervise bus children who come without parents?" Those who make evangelistic calls in an unofficial way make up another host of involved laymen who carry on the work of the ministry.

Dr. Falwell has a unique view of church meetings: "We don't want to have a lot of meetings, but those we do have should be well-planned, well-attended, and worth the while of those who come." As a result, the Thomas Road Baptist Church does not have as many meetings as most American churches, but those that are held are enthusiastically attended. Falwell maintains that a New Testament church should have Sunday school to teach the Word of God, church services to preach the Word of God, teachers' meetings to plan the outreach, prayer meetings to supply the spiritual power, and visitation programs to reach the community. Beyond this, Falwell states, most meetings in other churches tend to have secondary benefits rather than fulfilling the purpose of a church.

When special revival meetings are held, the members attend and become involved in reaching their friends. The February meeting with Freddie Gage witnessed a packed auditorium each night, with over thirty-three hundred present; and on the final night five thousand teen-agers were sitting on the floor, around the platform, in the choir, and standing around every available wall space in the building. The fourteen hundred decisions for Christ were the result of hard work and involvement by the members.

The members are involved in prayer meetings and Bible study classes. Falwell preaches that Christians should not smoke, drink, attend movies, or dance. The thousands who come continue to attend in the face of such preaching. Obviously, if everyone disagreed, the attendance would go down. But they don't. Therefore, their daily lives must be involved with the preached standards. This personal involvement is another reason for the greatness of Thomas Road Baptist Church.

A GREAT CHURCH PRODUCES GREAT CONVERSIONS

Greatness is measured by the changed lives of those coming to know Christ and the transformed values of those who sit under the ministry of the Word of God. The Thomas Road Baptist Church has more in-depth conversions that constantly take place than perhaps any other church in America. When Falwell gives an opportunity for testimonies, many individuals come to the microphone to tell of former lives of drinking, drugs, purposelessness, crime, and serving time in prison. The large number of transformed lives qualifies Thomas Road Baptist Church as a great church.

The alcoholic ministry at Elim Home is responsible weekly for men walking the aisles to receive Christ. These men with broken bodies and, many times, destroyed spirits, find new life in Jesus Christ. As Dr. Falwell travels throughout the south, he is constantly greeted by businessmen and church workers whose broken lives were redeemed through the ministry of Elim Home and Thomas Road Baptist Church. The pages of *Church Aflame* are filled with testimonies of those who have turned to Jesus Christ because of the preaching of the gospel. Each week at prayer meeting Dr. Falwell reads letters and testimonies of transformed lives: people from broken homes, drug addicts, potential suicides, and those who were redeemed from boredom and the humdrum life of American affluency.

The Thomas Road Baptist Church is changed lives, such as Joe Leonard, who received Christ in February, 1971, and poured hundreds of dollars of whiskey into the sink, threw away his cigarettes, and began actively serving Jesus Christ. The church is also made up of people like Amanda Horsley, married to a drinking husband, living on tranquilizers, and afraid to go out without carrying a small gun for protection. Yet her life was transformed and today she and her husband, Ray Horsley, are superintendents at the Elim Home.

George Hogan called himself a bum, rejected by society. He was in and out of jail so often that he could not remember the number of times he had been arrested. "One day as I was sweeping the jail floor I picked up a gospel tract, 'What It Means to Be Saved.' After reading this tract several times, I wrote Reverend Falwell asking him for help. Falwell referred the letter to Mr. and Mrs. Ray Horsley. They secured the court's permission for parole. The first week at Elim Home, after hearing the Bible preached and taught daily, I came under conviction, and, realizing that I could not help myself, I asked Christ to come into my heart and save me." From that moment on, George has been a new creation in Christ; "old things are passed away; behold, all things are become new" (2 Corinthians 5:17). Today, George Hogan is superintendent of mailing at the Thomas Road Baptist Church; his wife, Jeanette, is Dr. Falwell's personal secretary. But spectacular conversions are not the only ones; salesmen, clerks, and factory workers receive Jesus Christ in a quiet, life-changing way.

Dr. Falwell comments that most of the members who come into the church come receiving Jesus Christ as Saviour: "We have very few transferring membership from other churches, although we would be happy to receive those who are saved. I hope our ministry always is centered on bringing people to know Jesus Christ, rather than just providing a church home for those who move to the city."

A GREAT CHURCH MINISTERS TO THE TOTAL NEEDS OF MEN

There is another reason why the Thomas Road Baptist Church can become the greatest since Pentecost: research authorities would call it *synergism*. We in the church simply call it the ministry of the total spiritual gifts to the total needs of man. Falwell points out that the twentieth-century church must promote, organize, visit, counsel, preach, finance, teach, administer, and help the flock. He goes on to indicate that the church with one pastor has a minister who must be a jack-of-all-trades. We know from experience that the man who labors in all fields is master of none. Falwell continues, "In the Thomas Road Baptist Church we have specialists for every need of man and for every need of the community, hence giving a balanced ministry for all people." He explains that Thomas Road has a youth minister to counsel the teens, as well as pastors to visit the hospitals and to counsel those with personal problems.

Some may complain of the impersonal nature of a large church. However, these critics have never been in a large church. Falwell stated, "I honestly believe that the people in my church get more attention and a quality ministry because we are large and employ specialists." (The church has over three hundred full-time and part-time employees.)

The greatest innovation of business in the last twenty years is the development and construction of the giant shopping centers. Here is the synergetic principle of placing at least two or more services at one location to attract the customers. One major store in a shopping center usually will not attract the multitudes. However, a combination of services (providing competition and more services) of at least two large companies, with small supporting stores, has been the secret of the success of shopping centers.

The Thomas Road Baptist Church believes that the combined ministries of several agencies in one church will not only attract the masses to the gospel, but can better minister to each individual who comes. The multitudes will not only be reached with the message of the gospel, but Pastor Falwell deeply believes he can give a quality ministry to the total man for the glory of God.

The concept of multiple services is a practical application of spiritual gifts. "Every man hath his proper gift of God" (1 Corinthians 7:7). God has given different abilities to each person. One pastor is gifted to preach (1 Corinthians 12:28), another to counsel (Romans 12:8), and another to administer (1 Corinthians 12:28).

These gifted men are then led to a church where they exercise their gifts for the glory of God. The large church allows many gifted persons to use their talents and, in the final analysis, each member can receive more, hence grow more.

Thomas Road Baptist Church can become the greatest church since Pentecost because each ministry supports and contributes to all of the others, hence multiplying the outreach. "And in those days, when the number of the disciples was multiplied . . ." (Acts 6:1).

Lynchburg Baptist College has attracted young people from all over America who are soul winners, bus captains, singers, and ushers in the church. They encourage the laymen from Lynchburg, who in turn help to reach their neighbors. This year Treasure Island will provide free camp for over four thousand children; many will get saved and later attend Lynchburg Baptist College. Many children return home and reach their parents for Christ. The stewardship department has ten men who discuss with people their wills, annuities, and trusts, but these men are also soul winners. These men have been deeply touched by the Lynchburg Christian Academy and the impact Christian education makes on children in the community. Hence, each ministry at Thomas Road Baptist Church assists the other departments. The Thomas Road Baptist Church carries out the analogy, given by Paul, of the human body, where each member supports the other (1 Corinthians 12:12 and 14-16). This mutual help will enable the church to multiply its outreach, which can make it one of the greatest churches since Pentecost.

A GREAT CHURCH SATURATES ITS COMMUNITY

A final reason Thomas Road Baptist Church can become the greatest church since Pentecost is its philosophy of evangelism. Falwell calls it saturation evangelism. Few, if any, churches have evolved a philosophy of evangelism and been so successful as the Thomas Road Baptist Church, because few churches have made use of the mass media. Falwell explains his concept: *"Saturation is preaching the gospel to every available person at every available time by every available means."* The young preacher points to the experience of the early Christians in Jerusalem, who saturated the city with the gospel. The disciples were arrested and brought before the Sanhedrin, and charged, ". . . ye have filled Jerusalem with your doctrine . . ." (Acts 5:28). This insignificant verse is the key to the ministry of Jerry Falwell. He states, "We want to fill Lynchburg with the gospel." Therefore he takes the gospel to all people by all means: radio, TV, newspapers, Sunday-school busing, the alcoholic ministry, telephoning, jail ministry, organized visitation, brochures, and mailing. Falwell indicates, "I want to saturate the community and to saturate the conscience of every individual." He believes that every man at some time in his life comes to the end of his self-reliance and turns to God. The pastor states, "When a man seeks God, the Thomas Road Baptist Church will be there with the gospel, and we can help that man find God."

A young woman faced with a divorce walked up to the switchboard at the church and asked, "Is there someone here who can lead me to Jesus Christ?"

A young couple from Greensboro, North Carolina, when faced with divorce, drove to Lynchburg wanting to be saved. They believed what they had seen on television—that Jesus Christ was the answer to their home.

Falwell believes the key to saturation evangelism is (1) contact, (2) continuous contact, and (3) a consciousness of no limitations. Falwell believes the church should not be limited because of poor location, poor building, or what is felt to be a limited population. He states, "I found in Lynchburg, Virginia, a city of fifty-four thousand people, that there is no limitation to what can be done for God." Falwell gave an example: "When the church started sixteen years ago, we thought that five hundred would make a large church, but when we reached five hundred, we found ourselves reaching for one thousand, then two thousand, next three thousand, and finally five thousand." Then he went on to state, "I honestly believe we can average over ten thousand each Sunday in the Thomas Road Baptist Church." When the possibility of over-saturation was pointed out to Falwell, because one of every ten people in the city attended his church, he stated, "We can grow because there are many lost people in Lynchburg."

CONCLUSION

The Thomas Road Baptist Church is making more effective use of the mass media than perhaps any other church in America. Americans live and entertain themselves on gadgets that plug into the wall. In a nation that has spawned the electronic generation, perhaps we catch insight into the reason for the church's growth. But media alone will not create a strong, growing New Testament church. The message must be biblical, the outreach must be evangelistic, finances must be collected, buildings must be constructed, lives must be changed, and Christians must be fed the Word of God. In addition to media, the membership is mobilized to reach Lynchburg and the surrounding communities. Every available modern technique of advertising is used to reach every available person at every available time. The Thomas Road Baptist Church can become the greatest church since Pentecost because it puts it all together. The pastor, Jerry Falwell, is a man of God who has simply claimed by faith the promises in the Bible. Lynchburg provides unlikely circumstances and Jerry Falwell may be God's improbable man, but the largest church since Pentecost may be built on Thomas Road.

5

CAPTURING A TOWN FOR CHRIST

The primary reason Thomas Road Baptist Church may become the greatest church since Pentecost is Jerry Falwell. Jerry Falwell is the improbable man in the unlikely circumstances. He has already built one of the largest churches in America. What he has done in the past is predictive of what he can do in the future. His youth indicates he has many years left of service. Other large churches have reached their zeniths when their pastors were old, hence there was not time for further expansion.

Jerry Falwell, the son of a successful businessman, attempted to build a church in Lynchburg, Virginia, an unlikely place. Lynchburg was Falwell's home town, sophisticated by southern standards. The city's church background was dignified by church standards. Besides, many would think a home-town boy could not build a large church in Lynchburg because the Scriptures teach, "A prophet is not without honor, but in his own country" (Mark 6:4). Yet, the tentacles of the gospel reaching out from Lynchburg to the whole world begin in the heart of Jerry Falwell. His influence as a pastor, educator, administrator, and author make him a candidate for the title "the twentieth-century Spurgeon." The concept of saturation evangelism is the secret of growth at Thomas Road Baptist Church. When Jerry Falwell moved back to Lynchburg after graduating from college, he determined to reach every person in town with the gospel. Over the years he has used every available means at his disposal. God has blessed his outreach. The fifteen principles in this chapter reflect the ways Thomas Road Baptist Church reaches people for Jesus Christ.

1. *Pastor-led evangelism.* The Thomas Road Baptist Church was founded and is still led by Jerry Falwell. The key to saturation evangelism is the pastor. If a church successfully continues in the job of evangelism it will grow and ultimately have a great influence. Thomas Road Baptist Church is doing just that.

Jerry Falwell is evangelism through the Thomas Road Baptist Church, a gigantic congregation where fifty to one hundred respond weekly to the invitation and receive Christ. Jerry Falwell is evangelism through "The Old-Time Gospel Hour," broadcasting the gospel weekly through the electronic miracle of television over 456 stations. Jerry Falwell is camp evangelism through Treasure Island, where over two thousand children come for a week every summer, many receiving Jesus Christ. Jerry Falwell is evangelism through Elim Home, where men under the curse of alcohol come free of charge to receive spiritual therapy and renewal. Jerry Falwell is evangelism through Hope Aglow Ministries, where the gospel is preached to convicts in prison throughout the east coast. Jerry Falwell is evangelism through the Lynchburg Christian schools, giving quality Christian education to children and teen-agers in their formative years. Jerry Falwell is evangelism through the Lynchburg Baptist College, training and motivating young men to build churches throughout America, similar to the Thomas Road Baptist Church. Jerry Falwell is evangelism through the printed page, The Old-Time Gospel Hour Press, distributing five million brochures and pamphlets last year, and *The Old-Time Gospel Hour News,* a monthly newspaper reaching 540,000 homes. Jerry Falwell is evangelism through pastors' conferences, stimulating pastors to build superaggressive local churches similar to the Lynchburg congregation.

The Thomas Road Baptist Church cannot be correctly analyzed apart from understanding Jerry Falwell. He is the leader of one of

the greatest churches in America. He has been used by God to lead
scores of lost people to Jesus Christ. Robert Walker, editor of
Christian Life magazine, presented a plaque to Falwell which stated:

> America's Fastest Growing Sunday School, the Thomas
> Road Baptist Church, Lynchburg, Virginia. Sunday-
> school attendance increased by 1471 per week from a
> previous average of 3386 in 1970 to 4857 in 1971, as
> listed in *Christian Life* magazine. Presented to Dr. Jerry
> Falwell, pastor, September 1971.

In response, Falwell said, "In honoring me, you have honored all
of the workers of the Thomas Road Baptist Church, for without
them we could not exist." Even in spite of Falwell's humble reply,
every church worker knew his labor could not have produced the
present spectacular results without the leadership of Jerry Falwell.

Nothing stands in the way of Falwell's desire to build a great
church. He works fifty-two weeks a year without a vacation, managing to sandwich in one day or so a month for physical reprieve.
Falwell has been known to minister and preach all Saturday, then
drive his Buick back to Lynchburg, arriving Sunday morning at
6:00 A.M. He stated, "It's amazing how a soda can revive a man,"
then proceeded to preach Sunday morning, visit in the afternoon, and
preach again Sunday evening. Finally, he remarked on Sunday evening that he was tired. Also, Falwell may sit in a motel room an-
swering mail from 11:00 P.M. to 1:00 A.M., and finally open a Bible and pore over its contents for the next hour before going to bed.

Falwell's commitment to the work grows out of a driving conviction that people are lost and going to hell. Last summer, a middle-
aged gentleman in the cardiac section of the local hospital called for
Falwell. The nurse on duty stood in the door and would not let him
in the area. After a few minutes of verbal fencing, Falwell bluntly

stated, "If you don't move, I'm going to walk past you, because that man needs spiritual help and he has requested that I visit him." The supervisor of nurses finally arbitrated the argument and Falwell witnessed to the man and led him to Jesus Christ.

Falwell's deep commitment to the ministry is not measured by the size of a crowd. One afternoon he spoke to the Michigan Sunday-School Convention in Cobo Hall, Detroit, Michigan, that seated sixteen thousand. The following night he ministered in a small country church to less than one hundred.

During a Sunday morning invitation, Falwell directed a church member to a man in the audience. The pastor had witnessed to the man the previous week but was not able to lead him to Christ. "Go get him to come forward and receive Jesus Christ," said Falwell. The man did. Falwell returned home from a speaking engagement one night at 2:00 A.M. and in the morning made a call on a family that had just lost a teen-aged daughter. Time and physical limitations do not keep him from ministering the Word of God.

During December, 1971, Falwell promoted a My Heart's Desire Campaign. He had every person in the church write the name of one person for whom he would pray and work to get saved. Thousands of cards were turned in. Viola Pillow turned in the name of her employer, and two weeks before My Heart's Desire Campaign actually began, her employer walked forward to receive Christ as Saviour. She expressed deep appreciation for Falwell's helping her have more concern for people. Those who know Falwell intimately realize he will spend any amount of effort or money to reach people with the gospel.

Most preachers interpret "God's provision" as a supply of money. Falwell interprets "God's provision" as power to lead people to Jesus Christ. He believes the enabling hand of God must be operative in the soul winner's life to lead people to Jesus Christ. The lights in Falwell's office were on late one evening and a member of the church who was visiting dropped in to see him.

"I can't seem to lead anyone to Christ," said the discouraged layman.

"How many did you expect to reach this evening?" asked the pastor.

"You can't expect somebody to get saved every time," was the excuse.

"That's why you can't win any," reasoned the wise pastor. Falwell expects God to work in the heart of every person when the gospel is preached. His faith gets results. He sees sinners get saved every time he preaches.

Falwell also believes God will provide the finances. On Christmas Sunday, 1971, he announced to the congregation, "Pray with me for a quarter of a million dollars needed for television outreach." Half of the congregation felt he was visionary, the other half knew he would get the money because of his faith. Monday morning, he had a check for $250,000.

Missionary Don Stone had been called home from Taiwan because of the sickness of one of his children. Stone needed twenty-two hundred dollars for plane fare back to the mission field. Falwell shared the need of the twenty-two hundred dollars with the congregation and challenged them, "I'll give the first one hundred dollars; are there twenty-one other men who will give a hundred dollars each?" Men jumped to their feet all over the congregation. Within ninety seconds the money was raised.

Many have commented that the Thomas Road Baptist Church is people. Another went so far as to say, "Everything Jerry Falwell touches turns to people." However, to Jerry Falwell, people are not digits on an IBM card. He has a deep compassion for the thirteen-thousand-member congregation and can call almost all of them by name. The customers at a local restaurant all know Jerry Falwell, but less than 25 percent can name the mayor. After a church service, Falwell has time to speak to a millionaire who wants to give a large gift, as well as counsel the teen-ager who has a pressing problem. All the children in the church call their pastor "Jerry," even though the dignified members of the congregation attempt to elevate his position. After a crowded Sunday morning service, Falwell held a little child in his arms and stated, "If this little girl is not claimed in five minutes, she's mine." His love for all is apparent. Even though he walks onto the parking lot in a suit, he will stop to throw a football with the fellows and, according to their testimony, he can still throw a pass seventy yards in the air.

Seldom does Jerry Falwell go into the home of a needy widow without asking to see her Bible. He leaves a twenty-dollar bill in it for necessities. Alan Roberts, a student at Lynchburg Baptist College, broke his leg and was facing financial difficulties. During a pastoral call, Falwell left a handful of large bills on the night table. According to one businessman in the church, "Who knows the many thousands of dollars he has distributed out of his pocket in an unpretentious manner around this city?"

Falwell loves the sinner but hates sin. This is shown by his personal leadership against a proposed city ordinance for liquor by the drink. Yet, in the ministry of Elim Home his deep compassion is reflected for the forgotten man of society who struggles with alcoholism. Also, the jail ministry is proof of his feeling for men behind bars.

2. *Television evangelism.* "The Old-Time Gospel Hour" is viewed on over two hundred stations in every state of the union, and another two hundred foreign stations. A listening audience of millions attend church with Jerry Falwell each Sunday. Of course television across America will not build a great local church. However, the program is seen twice every Sunday in Lynchburg, and television saturates Virginia. Last spring, a couple in their sixties came forward to receive Jesus Christ. They live in Concord, approximately twenty miles away from Thomas Road, and will commute to church because they first heard the gospel on television. Other members who were reached by television come from Appo-

mattox, thirty miles, Bedford, thirty-five miles, and Roanoke, fifty miles.

3. *Radio evangelism.* Each morning at 9:00 A.M. Jerry Falwell chats with the city concerning what God is doing at the Thomas Road Baptist Church. He does not shout, as do many radio preachers, but rather gives testimony to the work of God at Thomas Road Baptist Church, ending the program with a Bible study. He has just finished a series on Genesis and is now entering a Bible study of Acts. Many Christians who do not attend Thomas Road listen daily to the radio version of "The Old-Time Gospel Hour." According to surveys, it is the most-listened-to program on any station in Lynchburg during that time slot. In the spring of 1972 the radio outreach had expanded from twenty-six to over one hundred stations.

4. *Cassette and record evangelism.* All the services at the Thomas Road Baptist Church are recorded on tape and made available to shut-ins in convalescent homes, servicemen, college students, and members who desire to purchase them from the office. The gift-offer albums have received wide popular acceptance. Each week Jerry offers a sermon and special music on 33⅓ rpm albums. He sits in the TV studio and announces, "This album is free to all, because if we were to charge, the very one who needs it most might not be able to afford it. The album would cost you five dollars if purchased in a Christian bookstore, but it is free. However, if you can send a gift of one dollar, three dollars, five dollars, or ten dollars, this is the way we support our work." Over seventy-five thousand sermon records are sent out with each gift offer, a good majority of them free.

5. *Sunday-school bus evangelism.* The church has seven full-time bus directors and two full-time mechanics to keep the eighty-plus fleet of buses in operating condition. The number of bus riders grew from eight hundred in April 1971, to twenty-one hundred in April 1972.

The Thomas Road Baptist Church Bus Ministry

AVERAGES

1971		1972	
January	— 593	January	—1607
February	— 689	February	—1764
March	— 722	March	—1884
April	— 753	April	—2006
May	—1084	May	—1887
June	—1255	June	—2278
July	—1224	July	—1880
August	—1232	August	—1462
September	—1503	September	—1885
October	—1559	October	—2176
November	—1708	November	—2211
December	—1562	December	—1902

6. *Telephone evangelism.* In preparation for a busy day, Falwell asked 109 people to come forward during prayer meeting. He gave each of them one page from the telephone book. Each one was supplied with the mimeographed greetings to use in asking people to come to Sunday school. The instructions read: "Hello, I'm Mrs. Jones from the Thomas Road Baptist Church. My pastor, Jerry Falwell, asked me to phone you to ask you to come to our services tomorrow. Dr. Falwell will be speaking on the subject 'Where Are the Dead?' He felt you might have some interest in this message and wants you to be his personal guest for his class in the morning."

7. *Promotion evangelism.* The church uses campaigns and Sunday-school contests to reach people. Falwell announced to the church, "We've got to get over these silly ideas that it is carnal to use promotion to win people to Christ." He went on to state, "K-Mart, Kroger, and A & P are in the promotion business and they

don't feel they are wasting money by running full-page advertise-
ments." Recently he offered a large family Bible to those who
brought ten to Sunday school. The spring Sunday-school program
featured the Twelve Disciples campaign, where each person who attended received a charm likeness for each of the twelve disciples.
The Bible lesson of the day covered the life of a disciple. A commercial artist, Gifford Akers, saved at Elim Home, drew a sketch
for each disciple, which was distributed throughout the Sunday
school. The sketch was printed on one of the church's seven printing presses.

8. *Printing evangelism*. This year over 10 million pieces of literature will pour off the presses at Thomas Road Baptist Church.
The gospel goes out by letter, postcard, newspapers, books, and
tracts. The church employs three full-time printers, and the ministry
of printing evangelism has grown to such an extent that now over
half of the printing needs are supplied by commercial shops. Falwell believes printing is one of the main reasons many visitors and
guests come to the church, aside from television, radio, the visitation program, the alcoholic ministry, and Treasure Island Youth
Camp.

9. *Camp evangelism*. Last summer three thousand campers came
free to Treasure Island Youth Camp, and over three hundred found
Christ. Children come from all over the southeast, from ghettos,
tenant farms, and middle-class suburbia, for a week of Bible teaching and recreation, all under a strong Christian influence to change
the child's life for eternity. Last summer over twenty-five small
churches that could not afford camping programs sent their children free to Treasure Island. This year over $100,000 has been
spent to modernize the camp and accommodate an extra two thousand campers. This $100,000 was spent on a new bridge deck
($25,000), new cabins, refurbishing the old cabins, new bathrooms
throughout, a new lounge, refurbishing the barn to accommodate

Sunday-school classes for weekend retreats, installing a mini-bike trail, a miniature golf course, and an amphitheater.

10. *Deaf evangelism*. The Thomas Road Baptist Church has the only comprehensive ministry to the deaf in central Virginia, providing free transportation and an interpreter for every service.

11. *Alcoholic evangelism*. Thirteen years ago, Falwell established Elim Home under the direction of Mr. and Mrs. Ray Horsley. Located in Amherst County, the dormitories sleep eighteen men and the Horsleys give constant spiritual care to the men who come for help. Restored men now live normal lives, thanks to the transforming power of the gospel. Some men high in the business field and others who are laborers thank God for the life-changing experience at Elim Home. The men from Elim Home attend every service of the Thomas Road Baptist Church and on many occasions help in mailings, printing, and maintenance around the church. Falwell and Horsley believe alcoholism is a curse of sin and the only permanent cure of sin is salvation and the power of God. Medical help is not given, but the men are involved in Bible study twice a day and have the constant counsel of Mr. and Mrs. Ray Horsley.

12. *Prison ministry*. The Reverend Ed Martin is an associate pastor at the church and a director of Hope Aglow Mission, an organized ministry to reach into the penal institutions of America with the gospel. Martin has visited prisons in forty-one states to preach, counsel, and follow up those who need the gospel. There are a number of former convicts who are members of the Thomas Road Baptist Church. Their transformed lives testify to all that the power of the gospel still changes lives.

13. *Education evangelism*. The Thomas Road Baptist Church has given birth to three schools. The Lynchburg Christian Academy, kindergarten through grade twelve, had over six hundred students this past year. Only 25 percent of the students come from Thomas Road Baptist Church. Some families who send their chil-

dren for Christian education have eventually been reached by the gospel and are serving members in the church. Mr. and Mrs. W. T. Lawrence sent their sons, Ted and Tim, to the Academy and in February, 1971, after a call by the author, Mr. and Mrs. Lawrence became members of Thomas Road, serving Christ in the church.

The Lynchburg Baptist College will be the secret ingredient that will make the Thomas Road Baptist Church the largest gathered congregation since Pentecost. Within the next few years, over five thousand students are expected, these coming from all over the United States. These five thousand students, plus the nearly seven thousand in Sunday school, with their wives and children, will multiply the attendance and enrollment of the church. Also, a staff of over five hundred will be needed to serve this four-year arts college.

The Thomas Road Bible Institute will become a day-school reality this fall. The Reverend Harold Willmington, considered by many students the best Bible teacher they have ever heard, will become dean. The Institute will have a two-year all-Bible course to prepare laymen who want to minister the Word of God and to prepare potential ministers who are not ready to give four years to college study. The Institute will have classes in Roanoke and Richmond and, through the use of the church airplane and television, will be offering classes in other parts of the United States.

If Thomas Road Baptist Church is to be the greatest, it must have influence. Falwell has a vision of students leaving the college doors, going out over America to build superaggressive local churches. He wants these churches to be like Thomas Road Baptist Church, employing saturation evangelism. Falwell honestly believes that his students can go and build greater churches than this one and have a more extensive outreach. One of the students jokingly said to Dr. Falwell, "How are you going to feel when I build a larger church?" Jerry answered, "By then I will be dead, the Lord tarrying. I want you to build a large church. But until you do, we will be the largest church since Pentecost."

14. *Financial evangelism*. One of the most neglected areas in local church ministry is the stewardship department. A pastor cannot build a great church without money. Christians must be taught their obligation to give their tithes and offerings to God. At the annual Stewardship Banquet this past January, $1,023,000 was pledged by the membership to the Thomas Road Baptist Church. Individuals turned in "faith promise cards" but did not sign their pledges, preferring to keep their commitments between themselves and God.

In addition, the stewardship department has twenty men who call on members of the church and viewers of "The Old-Time Gospel Hour" helping them to plan their wills, arrange for annuities, tax deductions, and the purchase of bonds. Many Christians are ignorant concerning their obligations to give to God. Other Christians are unaware of tax advantages whereby they and the church can save income to be used for evangelism. Expansion and outreach is made possible by the stewardship department. Its success is another factor that can make Thomas Road Baptist Church one of the largest churches since Pentecost.

15. *Commuter evangelism*. Several years ago Dr. Falwell was given a Cessna 310 to fly him to the many evangelistic meetings he held on the east coast. Before that Falwell would hold evangelistic meetings throughout Virginia, driving to a church to preach each night but returning to Lynchburg to carry out his pastoral duties. The airplane moved him into the commuter evangelistic field, enabling him to administer to the growing home church in his Jerusalem, as well as to reach Judea and Samaria. Three businessmen in the church purchased a $225,000 Cessna 414 to increase the range for evening meetings and insure greater safety to Dr. Falwell. The plane is radar equipped and has de-icer jacks along with a pressurized cabin. Last spring the church bought a $600,000 Convair 580,

large enough to carry sound equipment, the Lynchburg Baptist College chorale, and a team for evangelistic and television rallies. The plane is capable of flying nonstop coast to coast. One critic asked why the church should spend so much on a plane. In actuality, the plane costs less to operate than for the church to purchase tourist tickets for Dr. Falwell and the team.

Commuter evangelism has a twofold thrust. First, Dr. Falwell preaches evangelistic meetings, winning others to Christ and helping to encourage struggling local churches to reach their communities. At almost every evangelistic meeting a pastors' conference is held to encourage pastors from the surrounding areas to build superaggressive local churches. Dr. Falwell compared his pastors' conferences to franchising in the business community. "If we can help hundreds of churches learn the principle of saturation, we can duplicate the ministry of Thomas Road Baptist Church around America. I am not interested in setting up a business but distributing the franchise of evangelism."

The second purpose of commuter evangelism is the television rallies, held on Monday and Tuesday evenings in all parts of the United States. These rallies make new friends for the television ministry and encourage those who are faithfully supporting the television work through their prayers and gifts.

DANGERS TO GROWTH

The fantastic growth of Thomas Road Baptist Church is based on the aggressive leadership of Jerry Falwell. He is God's man and is the only pastor the church has ever had. Every new movement faces a serious threat during succession of leadership. Should anything happen to this leader, the growth of the church would be blunted. If the church found a new leader just as dynamic as Falwell the growth could continue, but change of leadership poses a threat to church stability and growth. Since the church is dependent upon his leadership, a two-million-dollar policy insures his life, with triple indemnity. The author has often asked the congregation to pray for the health and vitality of Falwell. Dr. Lee Roberson, Highland Park Baptist Church, Chattanooga, said, "Everything rises and falls on leadership." This certainly applies to Thomas Road Baptist Church.

The church has experienced rapid growth in new staff additions; over five hundred employees work for the church. The church staff at present has a deep determination to carry out the Great Commission. Most of them serve without thought to the forty-hour week; many give extra time. However, the history of institutions tells us that eventually, as bureaucracy settles in, form becomes more important than function. Even though an organization may be orthodox in doctrine, an internal corrosion begins eating away at spiritual fervency. If the Thomas Road Baptist Church staff becomes more interested in preserving its ministry than reaching out to win souls, it will begin to decay, ultimately declining in membership.

The people have rallied around Jerry Falwell and it is doubtful anyone could steal their allegiance. There seems to be no possibility of a split in the church. However, a split could occur if the people did not follow their shepherd as commanded in Scripture.

The deacons are among the finest found anyplace. They see their task of service as taught in the Scriptures. These men have followed Falwell's leadership and have never tried to usurp the role of the shepherd. The deacons will not hurt the growth of the church so long as they continue with their present perspective.

If the church changed its emphasis, its growth would slow down and finally reverse itself. The purpose of the church is to win souls. The unsaved come down the aisle every Sunday to receive Christ. If the Sunday school becomes an educational institution instead of an evangelistic instrument, attendance will follow the pattern of other deteriorating denominations. The primary emphasis is evangelism, not purity of doctrine, not purity of life. These are means to an end and when they become the primary objective, attendance declines. These last two items could hurt growth, but as long as Falwell is living, he should keep it all in perspective. Even at present, there are many pressures on Falwell to conform to the traditional American church. The arguments are similar to those in the Old Testament when the people requested a king because the nations around them had kings. But Falwell contends, "Why should we become like dead churches which are doing nothing?"

God has given the church a leader, and as long as Jerry Falwell keeps his physical and spiritual life, the church will grow—perhaps becoming the greatest church since Pentecost.

A bird's-eye view of the Thomas Road Baptist Church parking lot. This is proof of the effectiveness of Jerry Falwell's saturation evangelism—reaching every available person by every available means at every available time.

Above: Youngsters spill from buses every Sunday for Junior Church—where the action is. *Below:* Staff members help young teens sign up for Sunday school. Each Sunday a number of these young people respond to the invitation to be saved.

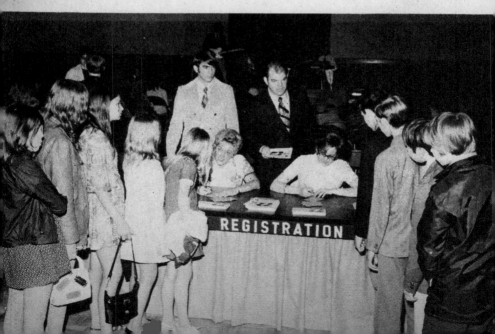

REGISTRATION

Right: Pastor Jerry Falwell—the primary reason Thomas Road may become the "greatest church since Pentecost."

Below: An overflowing crowd greets speakers at a revival meeting.

Above: The interpreter for the deaf gives the invitation to come forward for the Lord. Thomas Road Baptist Church has the only comprehensive ministry to the deaf in Central Virginia. *Below:* Dr. Elmer Towns, vice-president of Lynchburg Baptist College, and his wife greet incoming students at a reception. Within the next few years, over five thousand students are expected to enroll at the college.

Left: Members of Lynchburg Baptist College's first basketball team reach high to score. After graduation, these students will be reaching people for Christ. *Below:* Directors Mr. and Mrs. Ray Horsley in front of the Elim Home for Alcoholics, where care is based on the idea that alcoholism is not a disease, but is simply a sin.

Left: Daring feet in mid-air at Treasure Island Youth Camp, where children enjoy recreation while under a strong Christian influence. Many find Christ during their stay. *Below:* The annual Stewardship Banquet, at which church members are encouraged to tithe. The money is used by Thomas Road (and all of its evangelical outlets) to win souls for Jesus Christ. Falwell puts a biblical influence on money because "If you can get a man's pocketbook, you will eventually get his support."

Connie Smith, "the sweetheart of country-western singers," performs at the annual Homecoming Service. Seated left to right are Colonel Sanders, Singer Doug Oldham, and Dr. Jerry Falwell. More than nineteen thousand people attended, despite the hurricane which had battered Virginia two days before Homecoming.

Guests enjoy a dinner on the grounds of a local park on Homecoming Day. The dinner had to be transferred from Treasure Island, which was flooded by the storm. The rain didn't dampen the spirits of those who attended Thomas Road's 16th Anniversary celebration, however!

Part Two

MESSAGES OF THOMAS ROAD

The pulpit ministry is changing in American churches. The trend is away from the traditional authoritative sermon to conversational preaching or dialogue messages. The pulpit at Thomas Road Baptist Church is the secret of the church's greatness. The church has had only one pastor and preacher, Jerry Falwell. Even though he will invite great speakers, he still does most of the preaching. It is hard to separate a man from his message. Jerry Falwell puts it all together in the pulpit. He thunders "Thus saith the Lord," yet there is a sweetness so that parishioners say, "He is not bombastic." Falwell is quick to name sins—drinking and swearing. Sinners love to hear him preach because the preacher attacks sin, but loves the sinner. He always smiles in the pulpit.

People have tried to analyze the psychology of the pulpit at Thomas Road Baptist Church. But the secret is not found in oration or drama. The secret is not found in motivational technique or charisma. The secret of preaching at Thomas Road Baptist Church is the Spirit of the Lord. Only God can perform the life-changing miracles that transpire at Thomas Road Baptist Church. The supernatural blessing of Almighty God is the only explanation of the miracles at Thomas Road Baptist Church.

Seven sermons are included in the following chapters to illustrate the sermons used by God at Thomas Road Baptist Church. Some of these sermons are typical messages preached by Falwell on Sunday morning, Sunday evening, Wednesday prayer meeting, and one of his sermons is addressed to a gathering of preachers. A message Dr. Elmer Towns delivered to the annual Youth Workers' Convention is also included.

These sermons are included for more than illustration of the pulpit of Thomas Road Baptist Church. The preachers now want the same response in the heart of the readers as they originally expected in the lives of the listeners.

THE CHURCH AT ANTIOCH

Jerry Falwell preached this sermon to a gathering of preachers to motivate them to build superaggressive local churches. The biblical bases of Falwell's concept of *saturation evangelism* are found in this sermon. Although Falwell has only preached this message one time, the ministers who heard him have asked that he preach it often. Falwell believes that the characteristics of the church at Jerusalem and Antioch are the same that should be found in every American church. (His message on the church at Jerusalem is found on pages 34, 35 of *Church Aflame*, Nashville: John T. Benson Publishing Company.) Those who want to understand the success of Thomas Road Baptist Church should study the Jerusalem and Antioch churches, comparing the Thomas Road Baptist Church to them.

6

THE CHURCH AT ANTIOCH

I believe in the local church and I love my church—the Thomas Road Baptist Church. The local church is the most important institution on earth and it is at the center of God's plan when it centers on evangelism and the Great Commission.

I am not interested in the invisible church, wherever it is or whatever it is. I am not interested in some abstract thing that does not meet somewhere and have local members and a pastor and something going on of a tangible nature. I am interested in local churches, those that preach the gospel, win sinners to Christ, collect money, and send out missionaries. I am interested in churches that capture towns and spread the gospel.

Paul wrote to the church at Ephesus, the church at Philippi, and the church of Galatia. He was concerned about local churches. Local churches have been, and will continue to be in existence until Jesus comes. Therefore, the place we should turn to find God's plan to reach the world is the Book of Acts.

In Acts, chapter 11, we have the story of the origin of one of the greatest churches of the New Testament era. I say "one of the greatest churches" because the Book of Acts is filled with stories of great local churches.

The Book of Acts is the only book that has not been yet completed. It is still being written. The Book of Acts is the story of planting local churches, the embryonic stage of these churches, and then the spiritual explosion of similar local churches from town to town and from city to city.

It all began in an Upper Room. One hundred-twenty men and women met together and prayed in obedience to the command of Christ. After ten days, in answer to God's promise, the Spirit of God was outpoured. On that day of Pentecost, 3,000 more were saved, baptized, and added to that local assembly. Three thousand added to 120 made 3,120. And then God added to that 3,120-member congregation. Soon the number came to 5,000 men besides the women and children. That's a pretty good church when you have 5,000 members. Later they multiplied, and eventually history and tradition tell us that, before the persecution came, the church at Jerusalem numbered in excess of 100,000. Now remember, half of a city of 200,000 were professing Christians.

I'm using these statistics as a preface to what I am going to talk about tonight. It is my conviction that every local church should attempt to capture its city for Christ. Every Bible-believing, Bible-preaching, soul-winning church ought to attempt to win the entire metropolitan area to Christ. That is the prime objective of every church. We ought to try to win every individual, every soul, and every person, beginning at Jerusalem (our Lynchburg), then Judea (the surrounding county), and then Samaria (the state of Virginia for us), and ultimately the uttermost parts of the earth (worldwide missions).

My premise tonight is that every local church ought to be a worldwide mission center with its greatest influence at home. Our Christian and Missionary Alliance brethren have always done a commendable job. No one supersedes their efforts in the realm of world evangelization. They are effective on the foreign field, but with all the kindness I can generate, they have not done the job at home.

The first calling is to begin at Jerusalem and build a powerful superaggressive local church. The light that shines farthest, shines brightest at home. I think many independent Baptist churches have failed in their worldwide mission outreaches. I am not trying to condemn or to tarnish anyone else's efforts, but I am saying that to get missions into proper perspective, soul winning begins at Jerusalem.

The superaggressive local church that is getting the job done has one goal, one purpose, one obsession: winning its city for the Lord. If your church is in the country, you should have as an objective the winning of every farmer and every county around you for the Lord.

You should learn how to use the principle of saturation, which is preaching the gospel to every available person at every available time by every available means. The key verse for saturation is Acts 5:28. The church at Jerusalem was accused by its enemy, the Sanhedrin, of having filled Jerusalem with its doctrine: ". . . ye have filled Jerusalem with your doctrine . . ." The Jerusalem church had filled the city with its teaching. That statement was not the propaganda of some church public relations director. That was the accusation of the *enemies* of the church, and, if anything, was an understatement.

Seven years after the persecution that brought about the scattering of the great church at Jerusalem, Christians were accused of having turned the world upside down (Acts 17:6). They saturated their world without a radio, a television, a microphone, a printing press, or a television camera. Ladies, can you imagine living in a world without a telephone? They reached their world without telephones. They did it without airplanes. They did it without any of the modern means of transportation and communication that we take for granted.

The Lord said "beginning at Jerusalem," not ending there. The early Christians had become a little complacent; you cannot blame them. Can you imagine living in a town with one hundred thousand saved people out of a town of two hundred thousand total population? That would be a town where the people could *not* have voted in liquor by the drink. They had half of the town professing Christiani-

ty. They were evangelizing. They were evangelizing seven days a
week, and ". . . the Lord added to the church daily such as should
be saved" (Acts 2:37).

Persecution came, led by Saul of Tarsus, because God has a way
of reminding us when we fail to do what He tells us. He has a way
of reminding us quite actively sometimes. When persecution came
to the Christians in Jerusalem, they went everywhere preaching the
Word of God and planting local churches. Some went down to a
good-sized town named Antioch. "Now they which were scattered
abroad upon the persecution that arose about Stephen traveled as
far as Phenice, and Cyprus, and Antioch, preaching the word to
none but unto the Jews only. And some of them were men of Cyprus and Cyrene, which, when they were come to Antioch, spake
unto the Grecians, preaching the Lord Jesus" (Acts 11:19,20).
Now listen to a great statement, "And the hand of the Lord was
with them . . . ." (Acts 11:21). Do you know why? Because they
were preaching the Lord Jesus and they were establishing local
churches. ". . . and a great number believed . . ." (11:21). This
is not ministerially speaking. God does not exaggerate. "A great
number believed, and turned unto the Lord."

"Then tidings of these things came unto the ears of the church
which was in Jerusalem: and they sent forth Barnabas, that he
should go as far as Antioch. Who, when he came, and had seen the
grace of God, was glad, and exhorted them all, that with purpose of
heart they would cleave unto the Lord. For he was a good man, and
full of the Holy Ghost and of faith: and much people was added
unto the Lord" (Acts 11:22-24). Notice the word *added;* when
God is in a church, it is never static. If God is in something, it never
becomes stagnant. When God is in a church, you can tell by the attendance board. You can tell when you count the offering. You can
tell by the sinners around the altar. Our goal is to have God in the
church.

I notice across the back of this auditorium the mighty word *go* is in the word *gospel*. I notice on this wall that the goal for the adult class is 1,501 in 1971. Already by November you have won 1,590 souls to the Lord. When God is in something, there is going to be growth, progress, movement.

Barnabas got his hands into more than he could handle and he departed for Tarsus to seek Saul. He was trying to think of the next best Bible teacher around. When he had found Paul he brought him to Antioch. It came to pass that, for a whole year—twelve months —they assembled themselves together with the church. This church is not something invisible. This is not the universal church we hear so much about today; this is a local church. They assembled themselves together with the church and the Bible; they taught many people.

The disciples were first called "Christians" in Antioch. They never were called Christians in Jerusalem. Now they could be called Christians because they had been through the fires, they had been through the trials, they had paid the price, they had tasted the bitterness of serving the Lord, they had left behind their families and all that was precious to them to establish a local church. They had gotten under the Word of God. They were taught the Word for one whole year by Paul, the greatest Bible teacher of the day. Since the Word of God was not fully in written form at that time this was absolutely essential. And now, tested and taught, they were first called "Christians" at Antioch. And thus began the planting and organization of another great local church.

Let me talk to you about the ingredients of a superaggressive church. When I am talking about the church at Jerusalem, I always use the words *evangelization, edification, dedication, participation,* and *saturation*. Notice, the words may change and the features of any local church may change, but the church never changes. God is original, God is never stereotyped. God's ways are fresh and new, He is a God of variety; though methods and means and ideas change with situations and locations, principles never change. God's truth, God's message, God's methods, God's messengers must all meet the same criteria. So God's church at Antioch gets on with the work of evangelism. "Now there were in the church that was at Antioch certain prophets and teachers; as Barnabas, and Simeon that was called Niger, and Lucius of Cyrene, and Manaen, which had been brought up with Herod the tetrarch, and Saul. As they ministered to the Lord, and fasted, the Holy Ghost said, Separate me Barnabas and Saul for the work whereunto I have called them. And when they had fasted and prayed, and laid their hands on them, they sent them away. So they, being sent forth by the Holy Ghost, departed unto Seleucia, and from thence they sailed to Cyprus. And when they were at Salamis, they preached the word of God in the synagogues of the Jews: and they had also John to their minister" (Acts 13:1-5).

First, as an ingredient of a superaggressive local church, we find *persecution*. The early days of the church at Antioch were much like the early days of the church at Jerusalem, much like the early days at Lynchburg, or any other place—*persecution*. This church was born in fire. They had to flee for their lives out of Jerusalem and they came down to Antioch out of coercion—it was God *making* them go to the mission field in Antioch. They came to Antioch and they preached the Word of God everywhere and many turned to the Lord. A church was born, but born in the midst of adversity and affliction. Let me say this simply as a word of encouragement: Anything worthwhile, anything that has the sanction of God, costs a great price. Redemption came at a great price. Building superagressive local churches comes at a great price. Salvation is free, but delivering the message of salvation costs. It costs to build and propagate and deliver the message of the gospel. It costs to put up local churches like this one; you can mark it down, blood, sweat, tears, heartaches, heartbreaks have gone behind this work. There is no church in any town more misunderstood than the church that is, in the superaggressive fashion, winning men and women to the Lord.

When families are transformed, boys and girls are delivered. When you look around and see decency and dignity, honor and integrity, when you listen to the message and something genuine and powerful is going out, you can mark it down, there has been a price paid by somebody. That is the way it was in that day and the price is paid today. A superaggressive local church has got to be willing to pay the price of misunderstanding. Sometimes downright vicious attacks come from your own brethren. Sometimes the attacks come from those who preach the same gospel and who love the same Christ.

We've been in a bus ministry for three years; we started in November, 1969, and this past Sunday we had 2,155 riders on our buses. Four hundred eighty-eight came from one area of Virginia called Bedford. That is a little county seat and someone got mad because we were picking up bus riders in Bedford. We have five buses running in that area. We sent word to the preachers that we would like them to run some buses in Lynchburg, for nobody has a franchise on souls. "If three buses run down one street, one bus will get another you cannot get, and vice versa. You cannot overdo evangelism. Saturation can never be overworked. Evangelism is always underworked." Someone did not take that too nicely and as a result they sent word that they were going to declare war. They got the state troopers and town officers against us. Two weeks ago, one of our drivers got a summons for having the wrong color bus. They brought the ticket to me that Sunday morning. The officials had told the driver on Saturday they were going to book him if he came to town. So I announced that morning on the radio that some police officer in Bedford (our broadcast covers that area) had given a ticket to one of our buses for coming into town with a bus that was the wrong color. I said the reason I announced this was that somehow you must know that we have five buses in your area. All five will run next Sunday, same color they were last Sunday. We got another ticket this past Sunday. We are going to save them up for souvenirs. But we are going to keep running buses because 488 came out of that area last Sunday. When you are doing the work the way it ought to be done, brother, there will be persecutions, harassments, and ridicule—that's part of the price.

There is something else about this church at Antioch. Notice this preposition *in* (Acts 13:1): "there were in the church." You can't build a great superaggressive local church unless you have *presence,* unless the congregation congregates. A great church is known by great attendance. Some folks go to a football game or a baseball game and they will remain if it goes an extra inning, if it goes overtime, if it goes into sudden death; they'll stay until midnight or an hour later. But you let the choir sing an extra song and the preacher speak an extra five minutes and they will run for the door. You know why? Because they have not caught the vision. When God really gets hold of your heart, you will remain for the finale. You will stay till the end because what happens at the end is usually the best part of the whole service. That is when God gets His work done. In order to build superaggressive local churches you have got to have people present on Sunday morning and Sunday night and Wednesday night and on visitation days.

Last Friday night I was in Lubbock, Texas, and that is in the middle of nowhere. I hired a plane, a little Cessna 140. We flew down to Midland, where I got a jet over to Dallas and then I caught another to Atlanta and another to Washington. Our church plane met me in Washington. I got home about 9:30 the next morning. We had a full day, but I went to the church immediately. I got there and noticed folks coming in and picking up cards and going out. Jim Vineyard, sixty bus captains and bus drivers, had just had coffee and prayer together and were going out to charge hell with a bucket of water. Some visited till 10:00 that night and some went on until midnight—I mean going after lost souls, doing the job, because a superaggressive local church must have the presence of God's people. That is one of the reasons we have 9,235 in Sunday school on Sunday morning in a city of 54,000 people. We have 23 percent of the town already. That means we have 80 percent to go. That means we have a good foothold. That means we have just gotten the wheels turning. The work of the Lord in any town is just as limited as your faith and your willingness to work. No matter what church you attend, you are not limited by lack of potential, by lack of sinners to reach or by too many churches who preach the gospel in your area. If you had fifty or one hundred churches in Lynchburg preaching just like this one, all of you together could not get the job done before Jesus comes.

Presence is important. A pastor said to me, "I wish you would challenge the teachers here." He continued, "I wish you would challenge my teachers and workers on the importance of staying for church." I said, "I don't think they should stay for church on Sunday morning, I think they ought to get fired. Anybody that has to be made to stay for church on Sunday morning or to come back on Sunday night or on Wednesday night has got no business teaching. If a teacher does not attend church because he loves the Lord, because he wants to set the example, and lead the way, he should not be teaching."

I'm grateful for Lynchburg Baptist College. We teach loyalty to the local church. Many of our fundamental schools do not teach loyalty to the local church, but this is not true of Baptist Bible College in Springfield, Missouri. Many of our fundamental schools, though they have a good message, do not emphasize the sanctity of the local church. Sometimes we hire schoolteachers from other fundamental schools and we have to make them go to church. Imagine —we have to make them go to church. Sunday night, they complain that they have schoolwork. If I do not have time to eat, I still go to church. And if I have something to do I will do it at two o'clock in the morning, but I will be in church. You can always do what you ought to do. If you are a schoolteacher in a Christian school and you do not go to church on Sunday morning and Sunday night and

Wednesday prayer meeting, the Christian school principal ought to fire you because you are not doing your job and you are not setting an example. A church must have presence.

The third word is *participation*. "There were in the church of Antioch certain prophets and teachers." Barnabas, Simeon, and all these fellows were not only church members, but they were taking a part in the church—they were *participating* in that ministry. Participation is an ingredient in a superaggressive local church.

This is where training makes a difference. We always quote statistics that a certain percent of God's people do not tithe and a certain percent do not read their Bibles, and finally quote that 95 percent of God's people never lead a soul to Christ. You know why? It is not because these people are not sincere. I think it is because pastors and leaders in local churches are not putting forth the necessary efforts to train them to participate in the ministry. Every local church should have an intensive training program with the purpose of training soul winners.

At the beginning of the Jerusalem church, the members were all in the Upper Room. They continued steadfastly in the apostles' doctrine (the Word of God), in fellowship (church attendance), in the breaking of the bread (the Lord's table), and in prayer (the spiritual heartbeat of that local church). They were all witnessing. They were all daily in the Temple and in every house ceasing not to teach and preach Jesus Christ. Then when persecution came, they were all scattered abroad; where they went, all of them were teaching and preaching the Word of God. That is participation.

Why cannot all of us be witnesses? Do you know why most folks do not go soul winning? Because they do not know how to lead a soul to Christ. People feel incompetent; they do not feel they qualify for the task. Nineteen years ago I was converted. The first time I went visiting and knocked on a door, I stood there and prayed to God that nobody would be home. I will be honest about it. I braced myself for a number of months after I was saved for fear that I would be called upon to lead in prayer. I memorized a prayer, as a matter of fact; I had one all ready, and one Wednesday night my pastor called on me to pray. When he called my name I went into full flush and my mind went blank. For the next minute I said something, but I forgot the prayer I had memorized.

The reason God's people are not winning souls is because we are not training them. The Communists are training their forces. Sunday nights we have what we call an institute: The Thomas Road Baptist Institute. Dr. Towns teaches one course from 5:45 to 6:45. We have a prayer meeting from 6:45 to 7:30; we have had that prayer meeting for the last fifteen years. Our people come together and pray. We do not let anything violate that forty-five minutes. From 5:45 to 6:45 Rev. J. O. Grooms teaches a class on soul winning. We have another class on teacher training, on how to evangelize children and teach them the Word of God. Another class is on communication with the deaf, so God's people can communicate with the deaf community. We train people, by thirteen-week semesters, then repeat the classes over and over and over again.

Last Sunday there were 122 receiving the Lord as Saviour at our services, but many of them had already been witnessed to and many of them had been won to the Lord in their homes or on the job. Sunday they were simply making public what had already been transacted privately in their hearts. That is the way it ought to be —participation.

"And when they had fasted and prayed . . ." (Acts 13:3). The superaggressive local church is a praying church. Nothing of eternal value is ever accomplished apart from *prayer*. Nothing—absolutely nothing. Today, we emphasize automation and organization. I am grateful to God for all the innovations of this age God has given to us. In the midst of this population explosion God has given us the means whereby we can carry out His commission to preach the gospel to every creature. But in the midst of an organized society we must be careful that we do not become too hurried, too involved, too knowledgeable that we do not have time to pray. The praying church is going to see miracles happen every time it opens its doors. The superaggressive local church must have a good, sound, solid nucleus of praying people, who know how to get hold of God.

Tomorrow morning at 7:15, Dr. Towns and I will be meeting with the 120 staff members of our church at a breakfast. Part of the hour we will discuss the ministry and its various needs and problems. We will try to correlate and organize all our plans and projections for the future. Then we will have prayer together. We will commit the day, week, month, and the year to the Lord. On Monday mornings our pastors meet in my office. There we seek the face and direction of God. That means if we accomplish anything worthwhile, or anything transpires, it has happened because God has been in the act. Prayer. Nothing of eternal value is ever accomplished apart from prayer.

"And when they were at Salamis, they preached the word of God" (Acts 13:5). *Preaching* is absolutely an essential ingredient in superaggressive local church ministry. If you are going to build a superaggressive local church, you had better find a preacher. I was down in Texas recently and I spoke to a conglomeration of preachers. We had every kind. You could just name the church and we had one of their pastors there. One of the preachers asked if I had the baptism of the Holy Ghost. I said, "Yes, sir, nineteen years and eight months ago, January 20, 1953." He said, "Oh, that's great. How long was that after you were saved?" I said, "It was the same night I was saved. Same moment. It all happened simultaneously, and I didn't get part of the Holy Ghost, I got all of Him. I'm complete in Christ. My problem through the years is Him getting all of me, but I have all of Him." "Well, what you need is tongues." I said, "I haven't learned to properly use the English language effectively enough yet. There are lots of people I haven't gotten the message over to in English, and when I feel like I've gotten the job done well enough . . ." He said, "Well, if you could just get . . . ." I said, "By the way, how many did you have last Sunday?" He answered, "We had eighty-eight." I said, "You speak in tongues, I'll speak in English."

"And when they had fasted and prayed . . ." (Acts 13:3). By their fruits ye shall know them. The fruit of a Christian is another Christian. Now I am not knocking anything. You can talk in all the tongues you want, but do not do it at Thomas Road Baptist Church; it confuses things. I want our people to *know* what we are saying. I want to have a *certain* sound. God is not the author of confusion. Bob Harrington said before he was saved he spoke in tongues—vulgarity, profanity, and English—but he has spoken only in English since God saved him. Preaching is the plan God has used over the years to build local churches. The need of the hour is not coffeehouse dialogue and sharing. I'm so tired of these words —*sharing, communication, relevancy,* and modern lingo. When you start using these modern terms you are acknowledging that you have failed using the Bible terms. ". . . it pleased God by the foolishness of preaching to save them that believe" (1 Corinthians 1:21). You do not have to modify it, upgrade it, or describe it by new terms—just call it by what it is, preaching. It is not sharing, it is preaching. It is not dialogue, it is preaching. It is not talking in other tongues, dancing, walking, and yelling. It is not coffeehouse, conversational communication, ecumenicity—it is preaching. The ingredient of a superaggressive local church is powerful pulpit preaching. You show me a church that is getting the job done and I will show you a church where there is a preacher.

Dr. Towns has written for *Christian Life* magazine the article "The One Hundred Largest Sunday Schools." I think it is significant that this year out of the one hundred largest Sunday schools ninety-three are Bible-preaching, soul-winning churches. That ought to tell you where God is working. You had better get where God is working. It is not noise. It is not charisma. The word *charisma* is misused today. We hear so much about the "charismatic movement." That is a misnomer. *Glossalia* is the right word. Charismatic simply means gift of grace, and nothing happens more miraculous than what happens around the altar of independent Baptist churches every Sunday morning. *Glossalia* is tongues, *charismatic* is miraculous. When God is in something it is miraculous. When souls are being saved through the preaching of the Word, that is a gift of grace.

"And when they had gone through the isle unto Paphos . . ." (Acts 13:6). They literally went through the whole island. I mean they penetrated it. They did not just hit away at the fringe or announce their meetings in the newspaper. They went through the island. They went through it like Sherman went through Georgia. They knocked on every door. They saturated it. They filled that town with their doctrine. They won multitudes to Christ. Another word for their ministry would be *saturation*. Penetration or saturation is using every available means to reach every available person at every available time.

My mother is seventy-six years old. She has been around a long time. She was saved the second Sunday after I founded Thomas Road Baptist Church and she is still in the church. I remember my mother telling that when she was just a young teen-ager she saw her first automobile. Her dad said, "Do not be alarmed or laugh or you will scare the horses." Look at automobiles today, and think of the progress just in her lifetime. Some with white hair and some with no hair at all remember when there were not any radios around. When you finally got a radio, it was a crystal radio and everybody got together and listened to the "Grand Ole Opry" and a few other fifty-thousand-watt stations. I remember when television got here just after World War II. I was in my teens and as far as I know it was the first television set that came to Lynchburg. I found out who had it. It was the fellow who ran the grocery store in Fairview Heights. He had a daughter who was not particularly attractive. I started dating her and we watched television. I kept dating her until some better prospect had a television. Why is it that God has given radio, television, telephones, airplanes, automobiles, all of these modern media? Because God wants us to use them to saturate our city and our world. We must follow the example of Barnabas and Paul and go through the isle. God wants us to go through Lynchburg. God wants us to use everything there is to get the gospel out to everybody in all the time that is left. The Bible teachers? ". . . he which soweth bountifully shall reap also bountifully" (2 Corinthians 9:6). If you throw out enough gospel seed in enough directions, from enough sources, by enough people, and in enough places, you will have one perpetual harvest. For some there is sowing time, for some there is cultivation time, but for the majority there will always be seed coming in to harvest. "He which soweth sparingly shall reap also sparingly . . ." Five hundred years ago the printing press was invented. I think it is significant that the first thing printed on a printing press was the Bible. That is why God gave a printing press to us—to preach the gospel to every creature, beginning at Lynchburg and to the uttermost parts of the earth. Let us capture our cities for Christ. I mean literally overwhelm them. Let us do it through the principle of saturation, filling the city with our doctrine. And let us do it through the two secret weapons of a Bible-believing, Bible-preaching local church: (1) contacting people and (2) contacting people continuously. If you do that long enough, well enough, and loud enough, you are going to get everybody's attention. You may not win them all this year or the next year, but if you are willing to go to a church and invest your life and die of old age, you will win them one day. I am convinced that if I live long enough and well enough, the day will come when we can have 50 percent of our area saved and serving the Lord. Why not? In the meantime, with microphones, television cameras, and missionaries we can be taking the gospel to Judea, Samaria, and to the uttermost parts of the earth—all of it simultaneously.

Do you realize that every Sunday it is possible for any preacher in America, through the miracle of the media, to preach in one sermon to more people than heard Paul preach in all of his life? Why don't we get to it?

BECOMING A CHAMPION

"Becoming a Champion" was preached by Jerry Falwell at the evening service, April 23, 1972. The sermon was aimed at Christians, challenging them to go all-out for God, to become champions. Dr. Falwell had students of Lynchburg Baptist College in mind, wanting to motivate them to become champions. He took his text from the Apostle Paul's challenge to Timothy (2 Timothy 1:5). Dr. Falwell brought a framed picture of Vince Lombardi to the pulpit and during the sermon read from a speech given by the former coach of the Green Bay Packers on "Becoming Number One."

7

BECOMING A CHAMPION

Paul wrote to Timothy, a young man he led to Christ:

> Thou therefore, my son, be strong in the grace that is in
> Christ Jesus. And the things that thou hast heard of me
> among many witnesses, the same commit thou to faithful
> men, who shall be able to teach others also. Thou there-
> fore endure hardness, as a good soldier of Jesus Christ.
> No man that warreth entangleth himself with the affairs
> of this life; that he may please him who hath chosen him
> to be a soldier. And if a man also strive for masteries, yet
> is he not crowned, except he strive lawfully. The hus-
> bandman that laboureth must be first partaker of the
> fruits. Consider what I say; and the Lord give thee under-
> standing in all things (2 Timothy 2:1-7).

Paul told Timothy to be a champion. This apostle believed in
being the very best in his field, whatever that field. Before Paul was
converted, he was a man of letters, a brilliant man. Probably his IQ
excelled all the other followers of Christ in those early days. He was
a member of the Sanhedrin. He followed Judaism strictly and was a
Pharisee, a Hebrew of the Hebrews. He hated the Christian church
and, until his experience on the road to Damascus which turned
him completely around, he was the worst enemy of the church of
the living God. It was Saul of Tarsus, later Paul, who held the coats
of the men who stoned Stephen to death. He no doubt gave the or-

der for the execution. Paul was cheering them on, encouraging
them. Therefore, he was a murderer. He was at enmity with Christ
and with God, though he felt he was doing God a service. No one
excelled Paul in the business of playing havoc with the church of
the living God. No one! No one excelled Paul in the matter of letters—a brilliant man, a student who studied at the feet of Gamaliel
and who graduated from the University of Tarsus with honors.

When Paul was converted on the road to Damascus (Acts 9:4-
6) he heard the voice of the Lord saying, "Saul, Saul, why persecutest thou me? Saul asked the question, "Who art thou, Lord?" The
answer was, "I am Jesus whom thou persecutest." With that simple
answer, Saul of Tarsus was convinced that he was fighting against
Christ. He was convinced that the Christ of Galilee was the Mes-
siah, the promised seed of Israel. His reply was in the form of a
question, "Lord, what wilt thou have me to do?" He began going in
the other direction and he began doing so with all his heart. Paul
became the greatest student of the Word of God the world has ever
known. Paul became the most dedicated saint of the church age,
and I doubt anyone would question that statement. Paul became a
champion. Paul was a winner—a victor.

As an overcomer, Paul came down to the end of his road and
charged Timothy:

> I charge thee therefore before God, and the Lord Jesus
> Christ, who shall judge the quick and the dead at his ap-
> pearing and his kingdom; Preach the word; be instant in
> season, out of season; reprove, rebuke, exhort with all
> longsuffering and doctrine. For the time will come when
> they will not endure sound doctrine; but after their own
> lusts shall they heap to themselves teachers, having itch-
> ing ears; And they shall turn away their ears from the
> truth, and shall be turned unto fables. But watch thou in
> all things, endure afflictions, do the work of an evangelist,
> make full proof of thy ministry (2 Timothy 4:1-5).

Paul told young Timothy to be a champion in working for God.

Paul then said he had come to the end of his road. Paul said it this way: "For I am now ready to be offered" (2 Timothy 4:6). No doubt Paul could hear the sounds of the workmen's tools preparing the guillotine. Perhaps he could hear his captors marching down the hallways towards his dungeon to lead him away to death. Yet, Paul the champion could triumphantly say, "For I am now ready to be offered, and the time of my departure is at hand. I have fought a good fight . . ." (4:6,7). Paul looked on the Christian life as a fight all the way—a battle, combat, competition. "I have fought a good fight, I have finished my course, I have kept the faith. Henceforth, there is laid up for me a crown" (4:7,8). Remember, only victors get crowns. Paul was looking forward to "a crown of righteousness which the Lord, the righteous judge," would give him at that day; and Paul promises, "and not to me only, but unto all them also that love his appearing."

Paul wanted his young son in the ministry to be a champion. His letter was a challenge to the young preacher. We have Lynchburg Baptist College students here who are preparing themselves for some phase of Christian service. God wants each of you to be a champion. If you're going to be a Sunday-school teacher, a bus captain, a pastor, an evangelist, or a musician, be the best. No matter what you're going to be, God wants you to be a champion. He wants you to be an overcomer. He wants you to be a victor for God's glory. "Thou therefore, my son, be strong in the grace that is in Christ Jesus" (2 Timothy 2:1). Be a champion. "And the things that thou hast heard of me among many witnesses, the same commit thou to faithful men, who shall be able to teach others also" (verse 2).

First of all, Timothy, if you're going to be a champion, learn to multiply yourself by training others. A real champion is not a man who tries to do everything himself. A champion is a team member who knows how to function within the framework of a team. I've always been a fan of the New York Yankees. I remember the days when Mickey Mantle, Bobby Richardson, Elston Howard, and a host of others knew how to put it together. Although Mickey Mantle got most of the credit and a lot of fame, it had to be teamwork. There were nine outstanding men in the lineup, any or all of whom could hurt you at any given time. Professional basketball players, baseball players, football players—if they are really champions, they must work as a team. The champion is not an individual star but one of a team who knows how to function with others. The work of a superaggressive local church has to be the work of a team composed of champions. Men of God are not interested in being stars or gaining personal fame. Men of God are interested in learning all they can, mastering all the skills they can, acquiring all the maturity possible for the Lord Jesus and then manifesting, teaching, committing to others what they have learned from and of Christ. Verse 2 is sufficient justification for Lynchburg Baptist College. It's sufficient justification for teachers' and workers' meeting.

A little girl sixteen years old received the Lord this morning. She said, "I want to be a Sunday-school teacher. I want to do something for the Lord." The real dynamic of the Christian life who overcomes is one who says, "I want to be on the team". The man of God says, "I will be the best for God in the place where He puts me." God has some hands and some feet. God places every member of His body in the right place, and He wants everyone to function 100 percent. When every person is a champion, the job gets done. Paul told Timothy to learn how to be a member of the team and how to function at the maximum capacity in that place.

I think one of the greatest football coaches was Vince Lombardi. I always followed him with great admiration. When he passed away I had heard on television someone quoting Vince Lombardi on "What it Takes to be Number One." I began looking for the statement. My friend Freddie Gage said, "I know where there is one." A few days later I got a package in the mail. Framed for my office wall was, "What it Takes to be Number One." I've read Lombardi's words over and over, because I believe God wants every Christian to be Number One. Every Christian should head for the top of the ladder. Every Christian ought to be the champion he can be and ought to be for Christ.

Vince Lombardi said, "You have got to pay the price." Lombardi also said something else that is imperative. I hear folks saying that it is not really important to win. These people say it is just important that you play well. Lombardi said, "If it is not important to win, why do they keep score?" Of course it's important to win. But you have got to pay the price to win. Here is that statement from Lombardi:

> Winning is not a sometime thing; it's an *all-the-time* thing. You don't win once in a while, you don't do things right once in a while, you do them right all the time. Winning is a habit. Unfortunately, so is losing.

> *There is no room for second place.* There is only one place in my game and that is first place. I finished second twice in my time at Green Bay and I don't ever want to finish second again. There is a second place bowl game, but it is a game for losers played by losers. It is and always has been an American zeal to be first in anything we do and to win and to win and to win.

> Every time a football player goes out to ply his trade he's got to play from the ground up—from the soles of his feet right up to his head. Every inch of him has to play. Some guys play with their heads. That's O.K. You've got to be smart to be Number One in any business. But more important, *you've got to play with your heart—with every fiber of your body.* If you're lucky enough to find a guy with a lot of head and a lot of heart, he's never going to come off the field second.

Running a football team is no different from running any other kind of organization—an army, a political party, a business. The principles are the same: the object is to win—to beat the other guy. Maybe that sounds hard or cruel; I don't think it is.

It's a reality of life that men are competitive and the most competitive games draw the most competitive men. That's why they're there, to compete. They know the rules and the objectives when they get in the game. The objective is to win—fairly, squarely, decently, by the rules—but to win.

And in truth, I've never known a man worth his salt who in the long run, deep down in his heart, didn't appreciate the *grind, the discipline.* There is something in good men that really yearns for, needs, discipline and the harsh *reality of head-to-head combat.*

I don't say these things because I believe in the "brute" nature of man or that men must be brutalized to be combative. *I believe in God, and I believe in human decency. But I firmly believe that any man's finest hour —his greatest fulfillment to all he holds dear—is that moment when he has worked his heart out in a good cause and lies exhausted on the field of battle—victorious.*

The Christian life is just like that. The Apostle Paul fought his heart out. He paid the price. He spent the last days of his ministry in a dirty, filthy Roman dungeon. But he said, "I am ready to be offered. I fought my heart out. I'm lying on the field, the wind is out, but I've won the crown." The Christian life is to be a competitive, combative life and it's to be one of functioning, working, operating, and cooperating on the team which is the body of Christ.

"Thou therefore endure hardness, as a good soldier of Jesus Christ" (2 Timothy 2:3). First, learn to function as a team. Learn to cooperate. Second, learn to pay the price. If you're going to be a champion for Christ, learn to endure hardness. Life isn't a bed of roses. Paul wrote this from a prison cell. He wrote from lonely circumstances and said, "All my friends have gone, only Luke is with me." All the people Paul loved and who ministered with him had left him. He wrote, "Demas hath forsaken me, having loved this present world, and is departed unto Thessalonica; Crescens to Galatia, Titus unto Dalmatia. Only Luke is with me. . . ." (4:10,11). And yet in that lonely, dirty, filthy dungeon, Paul said, "Timothy, I want you to know now if you're going to be a champion, you've got to pay the price."

What is the price of being a great Christian? You are to be oblivious to what people think of you. The very moment you got saved, you thought everyone would pat you on the back and tell you, "Boy, you're a great guy." You thought this was the most wonderful thing you'd ever done. You went back to work; and instead of friends cheering you and praising you, they began laughing, criticizing you, and whispering about you behind your back. Your critics began saying, "It won't be long, he'll be right back, he'll fall; I'll give him three weeks." Then at home, you thought surely everybody in the family would be glad. But they said, "Don't take Christianity too far. Don't become a fanatic. Don't become a religious fool. It's one thing to be a good churchman, but you don't have to take Christianity to the extreme." You find opposition from everybody, everywhere. Opposition is part of this *hardness* you have to endure.

You won't always have the applause of men. You will have Satan as your archenemy. The moment you entered the family of God, Satan declared war on you. Satan is a roaring lion who goes about devouring those whom he can. The born-again believer is his prime target. Satan never relaxes. He never pillows his head. When you get up in the morning, the enemy already is there waiting for you. When you go to your job, the adversary beats you there. At night when you lay your head down on the pillow, the tempter is standing, waiting, watching. Satan is looking for every opportunity to knock you out of fellowship with God. He wants to get you spiritually out of gear. He wants to wreck and ruin your testimony. Learn how to resist the devil and he will flee from you. Endure hardness as a good soldier of Jesus Christ.

Also, learn that self is your enemy—this old thing called the flesh. I've occasionally met people who tell me they haven't sinned in many years, but any honest person knows that no such person exists. This old flesh is the enemy of God, the enemy of Christ, the enemy of holiness. This old flesh has to be dragged behind us anywhere we go for God. We have to pull this body—this flesh, this old adamic nature. It doesn't want to go God's way. The flesh can't live by faith. You have to endure hardness. Sometimes when you get up in the morning, you don't feel like living for God. Sunday morning comes around. You're tired—you've had a hard week. Every temptation and every lure faces you. Satan will suggest, "Why not stay home today?" Sunday night is church time, and you know where you ought to be. The old flesh says, "Aw, it's been a rough day; tomorrow is going to be one horrible day on the job. Why don't you just stay home so you can get a little rest? God understands. You're just human." Satan puts all these thoughts in your mind. Pretty soon, you've missed Sunday night service; then prayer meeting is a lot easier to miss, because you've worked eight or ten hours.

Satan knows how to tempt you. The time comes around to pay your tithes and offering. Financially, you've had a week of it, you're behind on your payments and you don't know how in the world you're going to buy the groceries or meet the car payment. It's school time, or time to buy a license, and time to put something on the car. You face all kinds of excuses, bills, and problems. You have God's money, God's tithe, and Satan tells you, "Why don't you hold it back for a week or two. After all, you need that car to get to church. After all, the children are a responsibility. You'll be able to pay your tithe back later." And soon, you begin stealing from the Lord.

The champions are those who endure hardness as good soldiers of Jesus Christ. Your tithe is the Lord's. Your time is the Lord's. Your talent is the Lord's. Satan, the world, and the flesh are all against you. All want to keep you from being a champion. You have got to learn how to put your face to the wind. No matter how cold, hard, or lonely, you must let the world go haywire. " . . . but as for me and my house, we will serve the Lord" (Joshua 24:15).

The third requisite for being a champion is found in 2 Timothy 2:4. "No man that warreth entangleth himself with the affairs of this life; that he may please him who hath chosen him to be a soldier." If you are going to be a champion, you have got to be single-minded in your training. No one can do two things well at the same time. You can do only one thing well. You can do two or three or five things fairly well. But you can only do one thing really well. God has a calling for you. If God calls you to be a preacher, He wants you to preach. If God calls you to a ministry in a particular area, that's what He wants you doing. If God calls you to be a student at Lynchburg Baptist College, He wants you to study. God has a call for everyone of us: Sunday-school teachers, bus captains, choir members, soul winners, ushers, or prayer warriors. We all have a calling from the Lord. Soul winning is our prime calling. A good soldier does not run off on tangents and get involved in sidelines. He does not get involved in things which may hinder him in becoming a champion.

It has been my blessed experience to read the biographies of men like Norman Grubb, J. Hudson Taylor, Adoniram Judson, and George Mueller. The one significant common denominator I find in

all the lives of God's champions is this—they were single-minded in
their training. They were not professional preachers. They were not
businessmen preachers. They were not involved in everything that
came along. They had been called to work for God and nothing else
meant anything to them. God's work was their prime calling. Some
of God's greatest servants get sidelined by money. Money can be
God's instrument for great accomplishment or it can be a stumbling
block that wrecks a preacher's ministry. The love of money (not
possession of money but the lust for money) is the root of all evil.
Many of God's choicest servants have been blessed with a little bit
of money and they've fallen in love with the almighty dollar. That
entanglement with the affairs of this world has taken preachers out
of the front-line battle. I visited a man in the hospital in Richmond,
Virginia; he had been a pastor and a very successful one. Love of
things got into his life. He was offered a promising job with an insurance company. He rationalized that money would make it possible for him to do a greater job in his ministry. This is a typical lie
that the devil can use. He rationalized that if he was with this job,
he would still be able to do his work and to pastor his church. It
wasn't long until he stopped preaching altogether. It wasn't long until his life got out of whack and pretty soon he was back to his old
habits. I saw him, long before he became ill, smoking. Of course,
that was just the first step in the natural sequence, a start going
downhill and backwards. Finally, I went to the hospital to visit him.
He had lung cancer. He said, "Jerry, if God should let me live, I'd
like to come to your pulpit and preach one sermon on Jonah. I
want to preach on the text, 'He paid the fare and went down into
the ship.' " Whenever you get your mind off the call of God and get
wrapped up in things, you always pay the fare. You always go
down. My preacher friend didn't get well and God didn't give him
the privilege of preaching that sermon. He did repent and he did
leave this world in fellowship with Christ. But his life, the light he
held for God, was put out. Once we destroy our influence for God,
it is very difficult to ever get it back. A good soldier does not entan-

gle himself with the affairs of this life. Love of money seems to be
at the top of the list of sins that wreck many of God's soldiers.

Another sin that destroys many of God's champions is morals.
We are living in an age of immorality. They call it the new morality, but it is just the old morality warmed over. There is still no twi-
light or gray with God, it's either black or white, right or wrong.
The Bible says, "Thou shalt not commit adultery" (Exodus
20:14). Yet today, we're being brainwashed by television, by Hol-
lywood, by the magazines of our day. We are being taught permissiveness and indecency. We are learning to accept the unacceptable.
We are learning to love the unlovely. We are being brainwashed
into thinking situation ethics is acceptable, that nothing is really ab-
solute, wrong or right. God's champion has to be careful in this
kind of atmosphere. If you want to be a champion for Christ, you
have got to remember the rules have not changed. You have to remember the devil still tempts through sin. Dr. DeHaan said a
preacher seldom gets over a moral failure. That is not just restricted
to preachers. This law applies to all of Gods' people. If you happen
to be a child of God and are married, one man to one woman, stay
that way. You had better remember that regardless of what he or
she knows about you, God Almighty sees, God knows, God keeps
the record, and a good soldier does not entangle himself with the
affairs of this life.

You may think I'm an extremist, but you have to be careful
about where you are and who you are with. When I'm driving past
a bus stop and see a lady waiting for a bus, unless I have my wife
or some other adult in the automobile, I don't pick her up, even if it
is raining. I may say, "Oh Lord, I'm so sorry she's getting wet," but
the Bible says to shun the very appearance of evil. My ministry is
far more important, my testimony is far more important than one
simple, honest act that may have no bad implications, but gives oc-
casion to the devil. The Bible says the accuser will take my good,
and cause it to be "evil spoken of" (Romans 14:16).

The Bible says no man that wars entangles himself with the affairs of this life. You have got to decide where the battle is. The battle is out on the front lines. Every little dog is trying to get you off the front lines to talk and to compromise. A good soldier does not get involved in all that monkey business while the work is left undone. We have a soul-winning job to do. Why should we leave the battle? We are doing a great work. The man of God who plans to be a champion must learn that he cannot be sidelined on tangents. Be single-minded in your training. Money and morals are the two damaging influences that too often destroy and defeat the effectiveness of God's champions.

"And if a man also strive for masteries, yet is he not crowned, except he strive lawfully" (2 Timothy 2:5). A champion must be a man who learns to operate and function on the team. He must endure hardness or hardship. He must be single-minded in his training. He must fix his attention on high and holy things. But finally, he must learn to live by the rules. If you expect God's blessings upon your life, you have got to live by God's blueprint. God has a perfect will for every life. You are only going to be a champion if you find the will of God and do it. There is no such thing as God's second will. There is no such thing as doing what you desire and inviting God's blessings upon it. Find out what God wants for you, where God wants you, then His blessings automatically attend.

Being a champion is living by the rules of life that God prescribes in His Word. You have got to carefully study the rules. If you watch the tennis matches or golf games or the basketball or football games on television, you know that winning has become a science. A player not only must have brute strength and a good mind, but there has to be that mastery of the science. A champion knows the rules to win. The fellow who goes the extra mile, learns the extra little bit, that extra something makes him a champion. The winner must have the edge to take him through because there is not much difference between champions and challengers in the world of sports. The same is true in the Christian life.

The difference between a champion and a defeated Christian is usually a very small thing. Sometimes, it is just a little cigarette that fills his pocket. A cigarette never put anyone in hell, but smoking has kept a man from being the champion that he could have been. He is hooked on a little thing, or maybe he never really saw the need for quitting. Maybe he never saw why he needed to be a daily, regular, faithful Bible student or why he had to spend time in prayer. Maybe he never saw why his dress, his demeanor, his hair, his testimony had to be disciplined and decent. A champion goes all the way. He obeys all the rules. A champion finds out what God wants and no matter how demanding, how strict, how disciplinary, he responds, "Lord, here am I, use me, send me."

D. L. Moody said early in his Christian life he heard a preacher say, "It yet remains to be seen what God can do with one man who is wholly surrendered to the Lord." Moody left that building saying in his own heart, "By God's grace, I'll be that man." Moody determined to be that man who was wholly surrendered to the Lord. He shook two continents for God in his day. I wonder what God could do with a church, a corporate body of believers who altogether said, "I will be a champion for Christ." I think we could shake the world for God. I really believe God is committing to Thomas Road Baptist Church, to you and to me, the opportunity of capturing a world for Christ. Are we willing to become champions? Are we willing to be Number One for God's glory? Are we willing to pay any price? Are we willing to make any sacrifice? Are we willing to endure any hardships in order to claim the prize? Being champion depends upon what kind of Christian you want to be. If you just want to be a run-of-the-mill, second-rate Christian, go ahead. But if you want to be a champion, listen to Paul. "Thou therefore, my son, be strong in the grace that is in Christ Jesus. . . ." Be strong in the Lord.

FEUDIN', FUSSIN', AND FRETTIN'

Dr. Jerry Falwell preached this sermon at the morning service February 27, 1972, with over three thousand present on a stormy Sunday morning. The predominant theme of the sermon, overcoming worry, was ordained of God because the congregation was not in its usual joyful mood, nor did it sing in a lively way. Dr. Falwell remarked after the sermon, "I know God had me prepare this sermon because there was concern written on the face of every person present." The congregation is usually responsive to the happy singing of Doug Oldham but this particular morning he noted a coolness and observed, "I don't know if it is the weather, Vietnam, or if anyone has a lot of problems, but no one smiled." Even when Doug Oldham sang his ever-popular "The King Is Coming," the people did not respond with their usual audible "Amen."

During the following week many church members remarked that God had prepared the sermon "Feudin', Fussin', and Frettin' " for their needs. Because of this overwhelming response, the tape of the sermon was placed on a 33⅓ record and seventy-five thousand copies were distributed to listeners of "The Old-Time Gospel Hour." It is once again recorded here for those who are constantly plagued by worry and are guilty of "Feudin', Fussin', and Frettin'."

8

FEUDIN', FUSSIN', AND FRETTIN'

Feudin' and frettin' are usually found among the hill people, but today I am going to show how God's people are guilty of frettin' and feudin'. The first word in my Scripture text today is *fret*.

> Fret not thyself because of evildoers, neither be thou envious against the workers of iniquity. For they shall soon be cut down like the grass, and wither as the green herb. Trust in the Lord, and do good; so shalt thou dwell in the land, and verily thou shalt be fed. Delight thyself also in the Lord; and he shall give thee the desires of thine heart. Commit thy way unto the Lord; trust also in him; and he shall bring it to pass. And he shall bring forth thy righteousness as the light, and thy judgment as the noonday. Rest in the Lord, and wait patiently for him: fret not thyself because of him who prospereth in his way, because of the man who bringeth wicked devices to pass. Cease from anger, and forsake wrath: fret not thyself in any wise to do evil. For evildoers shall be cut off: but those that wait upon the Lord, they shall inherit the earth (Psalm 37:1-9).

Life can be an adventure. Life can be a thrilling experience. Life can be one joy after another—or it can be a total and miserable failure. Some Christians give you the illusion that they never have problems, they never have adverse situations. Some Christians give the appearance that they never get *out* of trouble. The secret of these Christians is not in their own circumstances or their environment, but in the *attitude* they take toward their circumstances and environment. You are never going to live long enough to get out of trouble. Every time you get one problem resolved another weed grows in its place. God allows these problems. He knows how to keep us on holy ground. Some of us cannot stand too many good days back to back. We become self-sufficient, proud, arrogant. For that reason, God allows us quite often to enter that valley of the shadow of death. God allows us to experience some heartbreak, some disappointment, some backbreaking burden. God allows us to get under the load over and over because He knows pressure keeps us spiritual and trials keep us doing the will of God.

Too many of God's people are guilty of what David described as fretting. What does it mean to fret? The dictionary defines the word *fret* as "To give oneself up to feelings of irritation. Resentful discontent. Regret. Worry." That pretty well describes many of God's children, but it ought not to be so.

Giving oneself up to irritation. We usually blanket our feelings in some better terminology. We say, "I got up on the wrong side of the bed." That means we got up full of the devil, but we say we got up on the wrong side of the bed. Or, we excuse ourselves by saying, "I'm in a bad mood today." That means the devil has gotten control of our lives and our attitudes. We also pass the buck: "Things are going bad; nobody has it as bad as I do." That's simply saying that instead of being on top of my circumstances, I'm under them. We are not supposed to be under the circumstances, but on top of them. Did you ever ask how someone felt and his answer was, "Well, under the circumstances I'm doing pretty well"? And so such people resort to fretting, fuming, and fussing, and they become typical Baptists. Most Baptists fuss when they shouldn't. I don't know about Methodists. It may be that Methodists, Presbyterians, and Pentecostals have the same problem. I know something about

Baptists, because I have been pastoring a Baptist church for many, many years. I happen to pastor twelve thousand members here at Thomas Road Baptist Church. We even have a few fretters in our congregation, a few folks who fume—at least that is what the wives and husbands tell me about their spouses. As a result, instead of life being one spiritual adventure, it becomes a flop.

Why do Christians fret? David thought it was important enough to spend the thirty-seventh Psalm warning against complaining. David said bad attitudes can keep you from enjoying life. Your irritation can keep the people around you from enjoying life. No one likes to be around a sourpuss all the time. No one likes to be around a person who is always complaining—nothing is ever right, everything is always wrong. Fretting happens to you sometimes. We get in a negative state of mind. We become critical and vicious in our attitudes. We may not say anything, but our very countenance betrays us. We fall into a defeated attitude and our mood brings about failure in our spiritual relationship with God.

What causes a Christian to fret? First of all, fretting is usually caused when a person determines to have his own way, and fails. We are so full of self, that if we don't have our way, no one will! We complain, "If I don't get what I want, then I'm not going to do anything. Nobody's going to make me do . . ." Did you ever hear anybody say, "I'm my own boss, nobody's going to make me do anything. I'll do anything as I please"? When you start talking like that, the Lord is just about ready to cut you down. The very thing you say you will not do or the very thing you say you will do generally works in reverse, because God wants that old will broken and submissive to His will. When you find a Christian fretting, you can mark it down, his plans are thwarted. He made some plans, he made some determinations, he drew out a little blueprint of what he was going to do—and it did not work that way.

I was reading a book last week on being a successful salesman. The author was writing about getting the right attitude and a positive way of looking at life. He suggested we have goals in our lives and that we set deadlines and dates to keep those goals. That all sounds good, but the Christian life just does not work out that way. Quite often someone will ask, "When you first started the Thomas Road Baptist Church, fifteen and a half years ago, did you have any idea that there would be thousands coming here, six thousand in Sunday school?" What they expect me to say is, "Yes, I planned it all out. I knew exactly how we were going to grow. We had a goal for this year and we have a goal for next year." God has a plan through the years, as He has for all our lives, if we let Him use it. The Christian life is not plotting and scheming. The Christian life is surrendering and submitting. If you will learn the secret of surrender, as opposed to the futility of scheming, it will save you a lot of ulcers. It will keep you from being a sourpuss, a Christian weaned on a pickle. Surrendering to Christ will prevent you from being guilty of fretting, fuming, and fussing. When you think you have got to have your way, you are proving how immature you are. No one plans to go to the hospital, and yet a lot of good people do. No one plans to lose a loved one, and yet loved ones die. No one plans to have an automobile accident, a financial reverse, or a disappointment. No one plans to have some disastrous tragedy happen in his family. No one plans those things, but they happen.

The Christian who would learn victory over fretting must learn the secret of God's promise, "We know that all things work together for good to them that love God, to them who are the called according to his purpose" (Romans 8:28). We have no right to impose our desires on God's will. God knows best. Some of you are sitting here today and you have had one rough week. Everything has gone against you. You think the world is sitting on your shoulders. You think nobody loves you. That is not true. First, God loves you and I know that a lot of Christians would love you if you gave them a chance. But, your problem is that you have determined to have your own way, and God has determined that you are not. As a result, you sit down like Elijah the prophet under the juniper tree and pout. *Pout* is another good Baptist word. And so you have been pouting. God has got to knock that pouting out of you before you can amount to something. There is nothing worse than a pouting wife or a pouting husband. Every now and then a pastor gets called in on one of those pouting fits. It is a whole lot easier to get a drunk converted. You can easier get a drug addict off dope than you can get a pouter to stop pouting, because he enjoys it. That is part of pride. That is the old selfish nature coming through. "I'm going to have my way. I'm going to do what I please, and if I can't, I'm not going to do anything." So we determine to have our way and as a result we fret.

Another reason we Christians are guilty of fretting is that we calculate without God in view. We make our plans, we determine what we are going to do. Then we get on our knees and we say, "Lord, I want you to bless my plans." God has to be taken into view. The Holy Spirit has to be a partner in your plans. God has to do the programming and computing. God has to give the direction. And if He does, you can be sure He will bless your work. God is not going to bless while *you* make the plan, *you* plot the course, *you* chart the way, and then invite Him in as an afterthought. "Seek ye first the kingdom of God, and His righteousness; and all these things shall be added unto you" (Matthew 6:33). But first seek God, seek His wisdom, seek His way, seek His purpose. Too much calculating without God in view makes us fret.

I wonder how many of you have made some plans in the past week. You have plotted a course, you have made some decisions, but you have never prayed. You have never sought the guidance of the Holy Spirit. Too often we think the leadership of the Holy Spirit and God's thoughts are only involved in a local church or soul-winning ministry. We have a false way of dividing the sacred and the secular. We say, "Now, when it comes to my church work, I pray and I seek the face of God for teaching my class and driving my

Sunday-school bus, but when it comes to running my business or working my job, I know what I'm doing." You cannot be successful that way. God Almighty must be invited into your business, your home, your health, the raising of your family, your trips, your pleasure, your hunting, and your fishing. God Almighty must be invited into every area of your life or you need not expect the blessing of the Lord. God is not going to be relegated to a corner or a part of your activity. He is going to be Lord *of all* or He is not going to be Lord *at all*.

The reason we fret, fume, and fuss so often is we do too much calculating without inviting God into the picture. Faith is living without scheming. If you invite God into the picture, you will not have to scheme. You will not have to throw a fit afterward, because if your plans do not go through, you were out of His plan and He had a purpose in the failure. When your plans are His plans, you don't get frustrated if things fall into pieces. Then, the only time you will get frustrated and have your fits is when God had nothing to do with the plans and you failed, because your pride got hurt.

I'll tell you another problem. We must not calculate with a thought to do evil. Too many times we make our plans with some little evil in view. We calculate, we plan, we program; when we fail we pout. David said, "Fret not thyself because of evildoers . . ." Don't get upset because the world is getting rich. Don't get upset because other people are having it better than you are. You've got arthritis or a broken toe, and you're living right, while the fellow up the street who lives for the devil is in perfect health. He jogs five miles a day, all his kids are okay; he hunts and fishes half the year, and works the other half the year and makes enough to live on. Don't get all upset, or become angry because others leading evil lives are prospering, while you try to do the will of God and everything goes wrong. Don't try to rationalize why others have life so fine while you have it so bad. Others are always winners and you are always a loser. Don't worry about your enemies. The Bible says,

"Cease from anger, and forsake wrath: fret not thyself in any wise to do evil. For evildoers shall be cut off: but those that wait upon the Lord, they shall inherit the earth." Just because a man gets by with his sins for a week, a month, a year, or years does not mean he has gotten off free. God does not always pay off on Saturday. God always pays off, but not necessarily on *our* schedule. "Let us not be weary in well doing . . . we shall reap, if we faint not" (Galatians 6:9). You can be sure, God always rewards and blesses in due time, if you do not faint and give up along the way.

Don't try to chart your life, attempting to keep up with anyone else. Don't try to copy anyone else. Don't try to get back at anyone else. A life that centers around spite, malice, and jealousy is a life destined for total frustration and defeat. Don't try to keep up with the Joneses. Don't get upset when a neighbor gets ahead of you. Does it make you pout when a fellow employee gets a raise and you don't? Does it make you jealous when a friend gets a new car and you can't? Does it make you peeved when an acquaintance buys a new house and you can't? Does it irritate you that because somebody else seems to have more money than you have, he is a little more prominent, and the pastor gives him a little more preeminence than he gives to you? You begin pushing and driving, your whole motivation is to get ahead, outdo someone else, overdo someone else. You can mark it down, your scrambling will lead to fretting and fuming. You should stop trying to be anyone but *you,* the person God made you. That is all God wants you to be. Wait on the Lord. "Commit thy way unto the Lord; trust also in him; and he shall bring it to pass. And he shall bring forth thy righteousness as the light, and thy judgment as the noonday" (Psalm 37:5,6). You don't have to become anyone else, but you have to become what God intends you to be. If you calculate to do the will of God, you do what honors Him.

Mr. Loyd Adams and I were in Maryland the other night. A dear man had invited me over to his house some months ago but I

couldn't go then, so Loyd went. The man is almost blind. He wanted
to help our radio and TV ministry. He invited me again this past
week and I went with Loyd. We had a wonderful evening of fellowship. The man listens to our broadcast every day, and he told us the
blessing it is to him. He had some questions on the Bible. He is
eighty-three years old, blind, and lives alone but nonetheless he is
in love with the Lord. The average person would have a real good
case for self-pity, but he is enjoying life. He can't read but a neighbor comes over and reads the Bible to him. We left a copy of
Church Aflame and he said his neighbor would read it to him. He's
not complaining because he is blind. You stub your toe, you have a
great problem, you have a financial reverse, and you go into a nose
spin. You don't know what to do or how to handle the problem.
God Almighty wants you to learn that all things work together for
good if you'll take Him into the picture.

Finally, Christians are guilty of fretting, fuming, and fussing because they calculate for the rainy day. They feel they have to lay up
for the rainy day. That's an old philosophy and old philosophies are
not necessarily good. The Christian doesn't lay up for the rainy
days. He doesn't plan for the bad days ahead. He simply finds
God's will for his life. Now, I believe in insurance and Social Security, and I believe in taking care of your family after you die. We
have a stewardship department and we will help you with these
matters, and probably save you money. I'm talking about the old
boy who puts everything in a sock and robs God at his death. God
Almighty promises in Scripture, "my God shall supply all your need
according to his riches in glory by Christ Jesus" (Philippians
4:19). The work of the Lord will never get done if it is done with
the rainy day in view. Nothing of eternal importance will happen
unless the Christian goes by faith. ". . . the just shall live by his
faith" (Habakkuk 2:4).

A pastor who attended our bus conference said to me, "We just
can't seem to get a bus ministry off the ground. If we just had a lit-

tle money, that's all we need." I thought, "If you had the money
you still couldn't do evangelism because the lack of money never
kept anybody from the will of God." The lack of money never stops
God's work from being done. Lack of faith will always stop you.
Daring faith can put you in business for souls, but lack of money
never does. Lack of money can make you a prayer warrior. Lack of
money can make you trust God more. Lack of money can teach
you how to launch out into the deep and let down your nets for a
draught. But lack of money never kept anybody from doing the
work of the Lord. Lack of faith, lack of willingness to trust God,
lack of willingness to step out into the dark—that can keep you
from serving God, but not lack of money.

The reason most of us don't take giant steps for God is we calculate for a rainy day. We try to plan every step in case we don't
make it. We think of the escape routes in case we fail—I can do
this, or I can do that. But God doesn't want you to think of failure.
He wants you to charge the enemy with all your energy so in case
you can't win, you're finished. That's where God wants you, fully
committed. If you commit yourself to God, He will commit Himself
to you. "Commit thy way unto the Lord . . . Rest in the Lord, and
wait patiently for him: fret not thyself because of him who prosper-
eth in his way, because of the man who bringeth wicked devices to
pass" (Psalm 37:5,7). Don't worry about the prosperous fellow;
just prosper for Jesus. Get in the front line. Be the best Sunday-
school teacher in your church. Be the best Christian in your neighborhood. Be the best soul winner in your city. Determine to be a
giant for God. Stop pouting! Stop fretting! Stop fussing! Don't
worry because of what others are doing or have done. Don't worry
over what you have or don't have. Don't worry over what you do or
don't do. Start doing for the Lord! Start living! Start serving!

THE WILL OF GOD

It was at the evening service on February 20, 1972, that Jerry Falwell preached "The Will of God" at the request of the students in the Introduction to Christian Life class taught at Lynchburg Baptist College. Many students have testified that this lecture did more than all of Dr. Falwell's other lectures to help them find God's plan for their lives. As a result of the sermon a number of people came forward to dedicate their lives to Jesus Christ.

9

THE WILL OF GOD

The Apostle Paul wrote to born-again believers in the church at Rome regarding the will of God. He taught that God has a plan for every life, that every person can find God's will, and every person can perform the will of God. What Paul wrote concerning the will of God for those in Rome, he could as well have written to the church at Thomas Road. Paul is writing to Christians in his century. But every Christian can find the will of God here in the latter half of the twentieth century.

Paul writes,

> I beseech you therefore, brethren, by the mercies of God, that ye present your bodies a living sacrifice, holy, acceptable unto God, which is your reasonable service. And be not conformed to this world: but be ye transformed by the renewing of your mind, that ye may prove what is that good, and acceptable, and perfect, will of God (Romans 12:1,2).

The question most often asked me by mail and personal counseling is, "How may I know the will of God for my life?" Last Wednesday night, I preached on another phase of this same subject. I made the statement that it is absolutely impossible for you to know the total will of God for your entire life. I must repeat that because it is foundational in determining the will of God. You cannot know the total will of God for your entire life. There are several reasons.

In the first place, you don't need to know all of God's will for your total life. You only need to know God's will for *right now*. ". . . Sufficient unto the day is the evil thereof" (Matthew 6:34).

In the second place, if you could know all of God's will for your entire life, you would not be physically, mentally, or spiritually capable of accepting it now. The chances are that you would chafe at the bit, rebel, back out, and become a casualty. If I had known some of the ensuing problems twenty years ago when I became a Christian, I might have quit early in the game. God only allows us to know enough for today. At the same time He has concurrently provided grace to enable us to live through the day. As the old-timer says, "God never puts more *on you* than He puts *in you* to bear it up." If you have an impossible load tonight, God did not put it there. God will not tempt you with more than you can bear. Your failure is that you are not appropriating God's provision to enable you to live victoriously in all circumstances.

God does not want you to know all His will for your total life. He *does* want you to know His will for this moment of your life. These young people from Lynchburg Baptist College who just sang for you and the many others who came last fall to Lynchburg Baptist College did so because they believed it was the will of God. They have successfully—most of them—completed one year. They have fulfilled God's purpose for them in this one year. They have three more years to go. "Faithful is He that calleth you, who also will do it" (1 Thessalonians 5:24). That's the promise Dr. Towns gave them on the first day of chapel last September. God will complete His will in their lives, if they let him. They will come back next year, the vast majority, and several hundreds of others will join them. Yes, these young people want to know where God wants them. But they will not know the total will of God any more than you will know what God wants for you tomorrow. The Lord taught

us to pray, "Give us *this* day our daily bread. . . ." No provision is
made for tomorrow. God will feed you today because this is the
only day you have any promises of. You may be in heaven tomorrow—why do you need to know anything about tomorrow's provision? The Lord may come or you may die. Both alternatives are totally possible. Therefore, you do not need to make a lot of plans for
next week, next month, or next year.

We had some planners here a while back regarding the property
we have just purchased. They are making a campus development
plan and they said, "We have got to consult the pastor and get his
five-year projection." I said that was a joke. Five-year projection
—I have difficulty with five days, but not five years. The Christian
life is daily. Although I know what the planners mean and we are
working with them, at the same time the Christian life is full of sur-
prises. Living for Christ is the most exciting life in the world. I have
often said if there were no heaven and no hell, I'd still rather be a
Christian than anything else this world has to offer; simply because
of the joys we experience every day in Him, I wouldn't trade places
with anybody—anywhere.

The Christian life is the most exciting adventure in the world.
Nobody has the joy that the Christian has when he is in the perfect
will of God. God would not tell us to live in the perfect and acceptable will of God if it were not possible. By the way, God's burdens
and His yoke are not grievous to bear. God never asks us to do
anything but that He also gives us the enablement. He never says to
be filled with the Spirit without making it as simple as ABC so that
no one is left out for any reason. The common people followed Jesus gladly when He was on earth and for the main part that's the
crowd that follows Him today. You don't have to have a college or
high school education to know the will of God for your life.

Paul said, "I beseech you therefore, brethren . . ." (Romans
12:1). You must first be a member of God's family before you can
know His will. If you have not been born again, the first thing you

need to do is get saved. Come to know the Lord as your personal Saviour. Trust Him. Put your life in His hands. After that, you will find yourself on the road called the will of God.

Norman Grubb, one of my favorite writers, wrote that just as an unsaved man must come to a place of despair in his unredeemed self before he can become a Christian, a Christian must come to a place of despair in his redeemed self before he can know the perfect will of God. God has to bring you to an end of yourself. Sometimes that is a rough road. Sometimes it is a heartbreaking road. God has to take away your crutches. God must take away all the love you have for things that supersede your love for Christ. In order for the Lord to show you His perfect will, He must strip you of anything and everything that has preeminence over His Son, Jesus Christ. God has a way to do that too. God knows how to deal with those first loves, those obsessions, those things in your life that hinder you and restrain you from being the total maximum Christian that God wants you to be.

There is no reason for a Christian to live 50 percent of his life in God's will. God wants you to live 100 percent of your life in His will. There is no reason to hang onto the little habits or have little hangups, or be caught up in little idiosyncrasies. These things ought not to be present in your life because, "Only one life, 'twill soon be past; only what's done for Christ will last."

"I beseech you therefore, brethren, by the mercies of God, that ye present your bodies a living sacrifice, holy, acceptable unto God, which is your reasonable service. And be not conformed to this world: but be ye transformed by the renewing of your mind, that ye may prove what is that good, and acceptable, and perfect, will of God" (Romans 12:1,2). Do you know how to prove the good, perfect, acceptable will of God? First, you have got to realize whose you are. By the mercies of God, present your bodies a living sacrifice. You belong to the Lord. He has bought you. The Bible says, "What? know ye not that your body is the temple of the Holy Ghost which is in you, which ye have of God, and ye are not your own? For ye are bought with a price: therefore glorify God in your body, and in your spirit, which are God's" (1 Corinthians 6:19,20). We have been bought and paid for by the Son of God. If you are going to know the will of God, you have got to get rid of the attitude, "I'll do as I please—make my own decisions—choose my own route in life." You will not! You will not run your own life and please God.

I buried a man two years ago that God called to preach forty years ago. He determined he would not preach. He lived and died a miserable Christian. Before he died, he saw the loss of everything that was precious to him in this life, family included.

You will do the will of God or wish you had. The first step in knowing the will of God is recognizing who owns you. You are not your own. Thre is a missionary book out, written by a lady missionary, entitled *Have We No Rights?* It says the Christian has no rights. Our rights were all sacrificed in Christ. Our rights were surrendered to Christ when we accepted Him as our personal Saviour and Lord. We subordinated our rights to Christ and gave Him the power of attorney in our lives. Now God has the right to assign us to any position, consign us to anything. If God is determined that you will have physical pain all your life, as was the case of Paul, that is His business. If it is God's will for you to be penniless most of your life and never have some of the material things that others have, that is God's business. If it is His will and desire to send you to Africa, Asia, or some forsaken part of this world as a missionary, where you leave behind the luxuries and comforts that your family members and others are enjoying, that is His business: you belong to God.

Mahatma Gandhi asked some missionaries visiting him to sing a hymn for him during one of his numerous fasts. They asked which one. He said, "The one that expresses all that is deepest in your faith." The missionaries pondered for a moment and then broke out together singing,

> When I survey the wondrous cross
> On which the Prince of glory died,
> My richest gain I count but loss,
> And pour contempt on all my pride.

There's something glorious about the cross. Something that stirs the heart—that challenges the soul—that demands of the mind and the will total submission and dedication.

The first step in knowing the will of God is finding out whose you are. You belong to the Lord. You have no right to choose your own pattern for your life. God alone has that prerogative. Until you are willing to hand the driver's wheel of your life over to the Lord, you're never going to be happy.

One of the students in our college was talking to me the other night. He said, "I am facing a real problem. I have an opportunity to take over a large business and my family is pressing this upon me. They want me to say yes, and yet I feel the call of God into the ministry. They are against my entering the ministry. Financially, a decision for God will probably cost me millions of dollars in the long run. What should I do?" I didn't have to answer the question for him—I gave him just one look. When someone asks that question of you, all you have got to say is, "What do you think you ought to do?"

You belong to the Lord. You cannot, you must not, you dare not take orders from anybody but Almighty God. If God has called you to preach, you have got to do it. Young people often say to me, "I wonder if the Lord's calling me to preach." My answer is simply: "If you can keep from preaching—don't preach. If you can keep from going to the mission field—stay home. If God has put His hand upon you, He will make you a flop in everything else you try to do." The call of God is without repentance.

"Be not conformed to this world: but be ye transformed by the renewing of your mind . . ." (Romans 12:2). The second step in

knowing the will of God is renouncing this present world. There is a
positive and a negative pole on every battery. There's a positive and
negative pole in the Christian life. The positive side is, "I belong to
God and I willingly submit to Him." The negative side is, "I repent
of my sins and I turn from the world, the flesh, the devil, anything
that might have an attachment to my life."

The Christian life is based upon Calvary—Calvary's love. Knowing the will of God is simply knowing that He paid it all for me and
I owe everything to Him. God thought of me. He paid my sin debt.

When George Nixon Briggs was governor of Massachusetts, he
visited the Holy Land with three of his friends. When they got to
Golgotha, the three friends went up Golgotha to the top. At Calvary they cut a small stick from one of the saplings and made a
walking cane. When they got down to the governor, who hadn't tak-
en the trip, they said, "When we stood on Calvary we remembered
you and here's a little gift of remembrance." The governor accepted
the gift with gratitude and courtesy, but he tenderly remarked,
"Thank you, gentlemen; I appreciate your courtesy but I'm still
more thankful for Another who thought of me there before you
did."

The Lord Jesus has paid the supreme price for our redemption.
When you visit Calvary and realize in retrospect the price paid for
your redemption, you can do no less than give Him your best.
When you take that positive stand, you automatically take a negative stand against the world. The problem with many Christians is
they try to be like the old Ivory Soap—99$\frac{44}{100}$ percent pure.
They are willing to go most of the way for God. They will not take
that final step of commitment that brings the perfect joy of being in
the perfect will of God. When they take that step, money cannot be
the motivating factor in life. The Bible says the *love* of money—not
money, the *love* of money—is the root of every evil. As long as material gain is prominent in your thinking, you have not come to
know the perfect will of God.

There is a man joining our staff who is going to be head of one of our departments. For a number of years, he has been head of a department in a state university. He has degrees a mile long. He is a marvelous Christian. He has been pastoring on Sundays, filling in as a Baptist pastor for years. He is leaving behind approximately $20,000 a year to come here for about half that salary. I was talking to him in the office and said there was no way we could match his salary. He said, "You brought it up, I didn't." That is the kind of commitment that is absolutely necessary if you are going to know and do the will of God.

Beyond this, there has to be a renunciation of the pleasures of this world if you are going to know the perfect will of God. There are many questions you will stop asking when you come to total renunciation. You will stop asking, "Why is it wrong to do this? Why is it wrong to go here?" Once you have gone all the way with God, you will know what is right and wrong. The Bible says, "Be not conformed to this world." Anything that is conforming you—brainwashing you—molding you—shaping you to the ways of this world, automatically has to go. It is bad enough to have to live in any part of this world. We certainly do not have to go into the parts God has said stay away from. "Be not conformed to this world: but be ye transformed by the renewing of your mind."

You will also have to renounce some of the old friends. When God really saves you, He will not only make you love the Lord and hate sin, but He will make you uncomfortable around those friends with whom you once practiced sin. You say, "What am I going to do about my old friends?" You won't have anything to do about most of them. They will drop you. There may be a few that will come around and want you to have a highball or cocktail. There will still be a few problems. That is where spiritual backbone comes in. That is where testimony is involved. That is where you learn early in your Christian life that you can make no compromise with the devil. You are either with God or against Him.

How can you know the perfect will of God? First, you must surrender your body, life, soul—everything—totally to Him because of Calvary and what He did for you. Secondly you must renounce everything in this old world that brings reproach to His holy name. When you take that stand, the perfect will of God becomes clear and precious. You will understand the will of God as you understand when to eat breakfast and when to go to bed at night.

Coming to know the will of God is a subconscious thing. You have not been conscious of breathing oxygen since you came into this building. But you have been doing it and the proof of it is that you are still alive. You have not had to concentrate on breathing because your body is acclimated to it. You must have oxygen to live. The will of God becomes that simple and second-natured once you are in the right place with body, mind, soul, and spirit. Every person can know the will of God, can do the will of God, and can have a profitable life. Tonight, God is offering you a plan for your life. Will you take it?

"I CAN DO ALL THINGS BUT . . ."

This sermon was preached by Elmer Towns to the annual Youth Workers' Convention at Thomas Road Baptist Church, March 6, 1972. Over three hundred delegates were registered for the convention, in addition to the members of Thomas Road and college students who were present for this sermon. Approximately two hundred stood in response to the sermon, pledging to double their youth groups. Dr. Towns' first two books, *Teaching Teens* and *Successful Youth Work,* were written in the youth field. He served as youth director at New Brighton Community Church, Minnesota, and Southwestern Baptist Church, Dallas, Texas. Even though the sermon is addressed to youth workers, it could be applied to Sunday-school teachers or bus workers. The sermon is included to reflect how the ministry of Thomas Road Baptist Church motivates other churches to superaggressive evangelism.

10

"I CAN DO ALL THINGS BUT . . ."

Paul claims that he can do all things through Christ which strengthens him (Philippians 4:13). Can you claim that promise and do all things? Can you overcome a bad temper? Can you overcome worry and nervousness? Can you teach your children the glory of God?

We give many excuses why we cannot serve God. These excuses are given to our Sunday-school superintendent when he asks us to teach, or we may refuse to work on a bus route. We say "I can do all things but teach a Sunday-school class." We who believe the inspiration of the Scriptures with our hearts, actually deny it with our actions. "I can do all things but build a bus route."

Tonight I am talking to youth pastors. You are going back to your churches to work for God. Teen-agers are your mission field. Let me challenge you to build the greatest youth group in America. You may want to build the greatest youth group; but you need to make plans accordingly. First, set an immediate goal. The old proverb is right: "Blessed are the unsatisfied when they have a goal." Tonight I want you to accept the goal of doubling the attendance of your youth group within the next year. I want you to get twice as many youths attending as you now have. I want you to win twice as many to Christ as last year. God has promised to help you. The Scriptures witness, "I can do all things." That means doubling your youth group. But you confess, "I can do all things but double my youth group."

Mediocrity is the problem with the church today. We aim low and hit it with precise accuracy. May God give us an itch in our souls that can only be satisfied with success in the Lord's work.

"I can do all things but double my youth group." God is looking for great men to serve Him. The day of the gifted leader is not past. Just as God raised up the Apostle Paul and later Martin Luther and John Wesley, I believe God can raise up great men today. God wants to make you a giant. God wants to make you a prayer warrior. God wants to make you a man of the Scriptures. He wants to make you successful. Perhaps one man here tonight can testify a year from now: "I can do all things—I can double my youth group."

When I spoke at United Baptist Church, San Jose, California, Jesse Martin had 192 on his bus route that day. I felt that was phenomenal and wrote the story in *Christian Life*. Later Louise Seaton of the same church felt she could do better. Since records are made to be broken, she worked hard and brought 234 on her Sunday-school bus. Slick Goodman of Beth Haven Baptist Church upped the record to 334, and Gary Hinon of Central Baptist Church, Huntington Beach, California, now holds the record with 387 from one bus route. I maintain there are thousands of preachers who work full time in the ministry and are satisfied with a handful of people. Thousands of churches don't have 387 in Sunday school. Where are our workers?

Determine tonight, "I can do all things. I can double my youth group." Dusty Rhodes' father was a WPA worker during the Depression; college was out of the question. Dusty went to work with General Electric and became a self-educated engineer, winning many patents on his inventions. When he came to Thomas Road Baptist Church he used his technical know-how and piece by piece put our television studio together. Many of the parts came from surplus outlets. This quiet man has used his technical ability to reach over four hundred stations with the gospel.

The late Dallas Billington drove a fork-lift truck in an Akron,

Ohio, rubber plant. He was limited to an eighth-grade education. We might say "limited," as far as man is concerned, but God used Dallas Billington to build the largest Sunday school in America. Many of you have a good education, you have a car and money to work with, yet you complain of being unable to build a great work for God. You might as well say, "I can do all things but double my youth group."

God prepares the men he uses. Tonight I would like to explain the lessons you must learn if you aspire to greatness. These are the lessons you must learn if God is to use you.

1. *You must learn the success of failure.* Some of you will go home and fail at a task. You will have an evangelistic campaign or a youth banquet and the meeting will flop. You'll end up with egg on your face. How you react to failure will determine whether you will attain greatness. Failure is inevitable in life. All men fail at least once; many of us fail several times. What one does with failure determines his character.

Great men in the Bible failed—but they continued to serve God. They continued to work for God. Abraham is called a man of faith and two chapters in the New Testament describe his faith. Yet when he journeyed into Egypt, he was afraid Pharaoh would take Sarah for his wife and kill him, so in *unbelief* he compromised and told his wife to lie. Abraham couldn't trust God. He failed at his strongest virtue.

Moses is called the meekest man on the face of the earth. God called him meek (Numbers 12:3), yet when God asked him to speak to the rock, he cried out, "Must we fetch you water out of this rock?" (Numbers 20:10). Moses in an act of pride smote the rock with his rod and God kept him out of the Promised Land. Meekness was his greatest characteristic, yet he fell to a proud heart.

King David was called a man after the heart of God, yet he sought Bathsheba, committed adultery, then murder. David was known for seeking God, yet he failed by running after a woman.

Solomon was the wisest man on the face of the earth, yet he had one thousand wives. I don't call that very wise. Don't forget Peter, the bold fisherman. He grabbed a sword and was ready to defend our Lord. Yet a little maid sent him scurrying with curses and denials.

What am I saying? Men fail! They fail at their strongest points. The Scriptures teach, "Wherefore let him that thinketh he standeth take heed lest he fall" (1 Corinthians 10:12). You will fail, because you are human. So learn the lesson of failure. Get up and go on. Don't give up!

Don't look inside to your weakness, look at Jesus Christ. None of us will get much encouragement by introspection. "I can do all things through *Christ*." Don't look to your strength. Remember the greatest men in the Bible fell at their strongest points. Don't look to your strength or weaknesses—look to Christ. Remember Christ; He is the secret of success. When you realize your failings, rejoice— that's the first criterion of success. "For ye see your calling, brethren, how that not many wise men after the flesh, not many mighty, not many noble, are called: But God hath chosen the foolish things of the world to confound the wise; and God hath chosen the weak things of the world to confound the things which are mighty" (1 Corinthians 1:26,27). I figure most of you qualify for God's calling, because most of you are not wise, great, or famous. Therefore, go out and build the greatest youth group in America.

2. *You must learn the meekness of stubbornness.* One of the greatest problems facing Christian workers is balance. We tend to extremes. Many go off on the tangent of meekness. We emphasize yieldedness and passiveness. Don't pray to be nothing; God already has answered your prayer. Other Christian workers swing to the opposite extreme—they emphasize strong determination. We need both extremes to have a balanced Christian life. I call this the meekness of stubbornness. We must be putty in God's hands, yet determined as a ramrod concerning our convictions and Christian service.

The Apostle Paul had the tenderness of meekness. He confessed, "I have great heaviness and continual sorrow in my heart" (Romans 9:2). He spoke, " . . . by the space of three years I ceased not to warn every one night and day with tears" (Acts 20:31). Yet, Paul was not a tender plant to be stomped. He also was the oak that stood up to his friends. When his friends tried to persuade him not to go to Jerusalem, he stubbornly refused: "What mean ye to weep and to break mine heart" (Acts 21:13)? He cried out, "This *one* thing I do" (Philippians 3:13), not these forty things I dabble in. Paul had a strong will. It's said that many Christians magnify the cream puff and reject the man with a ramrod for a backbone. The truly great man has balanced both extremes in his heart—meekness and stubbornness.

You must have a hard head to be a youth leader. People will tell you that your young people want parties but don't like to pray. Don't believe what your carnal counselors tell you. Be true to your convictions. Be firm in your plans. There is a difference between New Testament youth work and relevant youth work. A leader must go on with his plans in spite of all obstacles.

Winston Churchill is one of my favorite authors, and I read his works with respect. I think he will be recognized by historians as one of the greatest leaders of our century. His indomitable will inspired the English to resist Hitler when Neville Chamberlain sought appeasement. When Hitler's war machine threatened to steamroll the almost defenseless island, Churchill thundered, "We will fight on the beaches, we will fight in the fields, we will fight in the streets." After staying awake all night in the war room, Churchill was driven through the still burning fires of London from the previous night's air raids. He was reading the list of RAF boys killed, and grief should have sapped his drive. The prime minister was ushered into a schoolroom to address fifth-grade children. The room's ceiling was partly missing. Facing the futility of it all, he thundered "We will never, never, *never* give up!" With that, he turned and walked out. We need that determination in the Lord's work. Never give up. Never stop winning souls. Never turn back.

Dr. Bob Gray of Jacksonville Baptist Temple tells the story of a lady bus captain who brings more than seventy children to Sunday school each week. She has multiple sclerosis, yet drives out to her route. She gets the wheelchair out of the car and wheels herself through the neighborhood, inviting children to Sunday school. That's determination. When she comes to a house with a terrace or stairs, she yells till the people come to the door. That's stubbornness. Some of you ought to go back to your churches with the meekness of stubbornness to double the attendance of your youth groups.

3. *You need to learn the opportunity of obstacles.* Life was not created without obstacles. Every garden has its weeds and every person has a sinful nature. Life would be simple if every man sought the good for his fellowman. But the lust of the flesh, the lust of the eyes and the pride of life are barriers to God's blessings. When you work with teens you will have heartaches and headaches. The best will break your heart and the worst will crush your spirit. You will attempt to get them to live holy lives, but they won't. You will attempt to get them to win souls, but they won't. You can't build a great youth group without the help of your kids. They won't help your cause. They will hurt it. You will have obstacles defeating your spirit. How you handle obstacles will determine your greatness.

Mountains in the Bible symbolize obstacles. They were barriers to the travelers and were useless to the farmers. After Caleb helped Joshua conquer the promised land, he had the right to choose a homestead. He chose Mount Hebron, even though the Anakims dwelt there. Caleb was eighty-five years old and should have retired in a protective shelter. Caleb chose a difficult thing. He asked God to give him a mountain, an obstacle. Why don't you ask God for a difficult thing? Why don't you ask God to double your youth group?

Then, like Caleb, go out and fight the enemy, win the battle. We don't have great victories for God because we don't ask for them.

We have been raised in an easy world. Things that come easy are not usually appreciated. There is an old Chinese proverb, "You can't carve rotten wood." We need strength of character, toughness of fiber. Then God can carve upon us and make us into instruments He can use.

Learn to rise above your obstacles, rather than let them defeat you. Look at the ring on your finger. It's probably gold. Precious gold was just ore with no comeliness, but it went through the refiner's fire to be precious. Your present suffering may be the refiner's fire to make your life pure. Each of you married ladies has a diamond on your finger. It would be just another piece of coal, if it had not undergone tremendous pressure in the heart of the earth. The more pressure, the better the diamond. The pressure you now experience may be sent by God to make you a stalwart man of God. You ladies splash on perfume, we men use it in after-shave lotion. The sweet fragrance once resided in the flower, but the petals were crushed and from the grinding wheels of determination came the sweetness of perfume. You may now be in the grinding wheels of pressure. Is God behind the process? Is He the determination behind the obstacles that overwhelm you?

You give excuses. "I can do all things but double my youth group." You complain about not having enough money. You are bitter about your pastoral leadership, or lack of it. You grumble because of poor facilities. No one will give you the perfect situation to serve Christ; the ministry does not come on a silver platter. You go and win teens to Christ, then these spiritual babes in Christ break your heart. You have to raise money and beg for better facilities. You have to plan meetings and teach lessons, only to have young people stay home, those who most need your wisdom. You counsel your flock, time and again, only to see a young girl marry an unsaved boy. Your heart will be broken when they mess up their lives.

You complain, then go home and lick your sores. You rationalize, "The kids won't follow me, so I'll quit." No! Go on praying, working, counseling, preaching, planning, and hoping. If you faint not, you can build the greatest youth department. If you can overcome obstacles, you can see young men go from your church to become pastors, foreign missionaries, and teachers in Christian schools. Listen, the lives of your kids are worth the trouble of overcoming obstacles.

4. *You must learn the potential of people.* All too often we accept man for what he is, rather than realize what God can do for him. We never think of the transforming grace of God when we see a smart-aleck kid with long hair, a big mouth, and a stubborn will. Remember, don't judge teens for what they are. You must have faith in the power of God and believe that God can transform any life. A youth pastor must have a knowledge of adolescent psychology. You must know teens, but don't worship at the shrine of behaviorism. Any social worker will tell you the limits of human nature. They work with the forces of human nature to help teens better themselves. You have a higher commitment. You begin at the level of the social worker; you must know the nature of adolescence. But go on to a supernatural dynamic. Only God changes lives. God changes any life that will sincerely repent and turn in faith to Jesus Christ.

John was the youngest disciple and impatience is the failing of youth. When Jesus went through Samaria, young John wanted to bring fire out of heaven because the people there didn't receive his Lord. John was similar to many of you—he had a chip on his shoulder. You are purist; you expect all things to be perfect and you fly into a rage when they are not. But Jesus did not judge John for his youthful intemperance. Our Lord knew what the grace of God could do for the young man. Later John became the patriarch of the apostles. He wrote, "My little children, these things write I unto you, that ye sin not" (1 John 2:1). Do you believe God can make pastors out of some of your youthful hotheads? If not, you ought to ask God to give you faith to trust Him for miracles in the lives of your kids.

Self-righteous men brought to Jesus a prostitute of the streets. There is no one lower than a whore. Yet, Christ didn't judge her for what she was, He knew what she could become.

What is your attitude when counseling a girl who confesses pre-martial sex, or even the girl who had an illegitimate child? Are you overwhelmed by her sin? Or do you have great confidence in the power of God to restore a fallen girl and transform her life?

Matthew was a hated tax collector, ostrasized and despised. Yet Christ entrusted him with writing the Gospel of Matthew.

What is your attitude toward a teen who has been arrested? Do you believe God can change a hardened criminal?

When Christ saw Peter coming, he named him *Cephas,* which is translated, "a stone." *Stone* means firm or solid. But Peter was anything but firm or stable. Peter was sand; he was as instable as the shifting beach. He vowed never to leave the Lord, and later denied Him three times. He told the Lord he would never permit Him to wash his feet, then begged to be washed all over.

Do you have young people in your group that are unreliable? They promise to make a poster for a program, then don't even show up. You need to learn the potential of people. God can make an unreliable teen into a faithful soul winner. God changes lives; that's what the ministry is all about.

Some of you complain about the carnal teens in your church. You maintain your teens don't know their Bible. They don't pray. They don't go soul winning. They don't care. Whose fault is that? You have what you work for. You are the fault. If you believe God can change their lives, this belief comes out of a deep settled confidence in the Word of God. Go out to put the Bible to work in their lives.

The size of your God determines the size of your faith. The size of your faith determines the size of your youth group. If you have a puny God, you will have a small youth group. If you have a powerless God, you will only have a club meeting in a church. My God created the world out of nothing. My God created man out of the dust of the earth. My God pushed the Red Sea back and one million Israelities walked across on dry land. My God arose out of the grave on that first Easter Sunday morning. The miracles of the past can be performed now. God can transform the lives of young people. God can transform the lives of youth pastors. God can build a great youth work, if you will let Him. You must have the faith to trust God for great things.

When Christ wanted to feed the multitude of five thousand people there was no food available. A small lad had only five barley loaves and two small fishes. Our Lord faced an impossible task. He had *inadequate resources;* the fish and bread would never feed the multitude. He had *limited circumstances;* there was no place to turn for food—they were in a wilderness. He only had *unlikely people* to help him. The small lad was surely not a catering service. Here we learn that man's need is God's supply. Christ fed the multitude. There are thousands of teens in your neighborhood. Christ wants you to give them the bread of life.

You give the excuse of *inadequate resources.* You say that your budget is small, your youth rooms are poorly equipped, or the church is on the wrong side of town. You say, "I can do all things but double my youth group."

You give the excuse of *limited circumstances.* You rationalize that your kids are unspiritual. You complain about the poor program in the rest of the church or the unsympathetic adults. You say, "I can do all things but double my youth work."

You give the excuse of *unlikely people.* You may think your pastor is second-rate. You may have no confidence in yourself. You may complain about your lack of education or your lack of Bible knowledge. You say, "I can do all things but double my youth group."

Start tonight and learn the lessons of great men. Learn from your failure. You will probably fail at your strongest point, but get up and put your failure under the blood of Christ; resolve never to repeat that mistake again.

Learn the meekness of stubbornness. Always be sensitive to the Lord and have compassion for the souls of men. Yet, be stubborn for the fundamentals of the faith. Be stubborn for the program of evangelism. Be hardheaded in your loyalty to your church.

Learn the opportunity of obstacles. Satan is going to try to discourage you. Sin will try to defeat you. Your own sinful nature will resist efforts to serve God. All these obstacles will militate against you. Name your obstacles. Now ask God to give you victory over the obstacles. Remember, God has a purpose in the obstacles. Find this purpose and apply the lessons to your life.

Learn the potential of people. Every person has a great potential, if only he will follow God's Word. Every man can be transofrmed if he will apply the power of God to his life. Every teen in your church has a great potential in God's service. Help him find the secret to Christian service.

Do you want to double your youth group? If you double the output, you will have to double the input. You will have to double your visitation, double your efforts, double your advertisement, double your prayer life. You have to do something, not just sit there.

The disciples were in a boat on the Sea of Galilee and a storm raged. They cried out for fear of losing their lives. When they saw the Lord walking on the water, Peter yelled, "Lord, if it be thou, bid me come."

"Come," said the Lord.

Peter did what no man ever did in the past and has never done in the future; he walked on the water. He did the impossible. There were twelve men in the boat, but only one ventured in faith and walked on water. Eleven men were boat-sitters. They didn't step out and even try to walk on water. Tonight we have some water-walkers here. You are going to step out for God and do the impossible. You are going to spend money, instigate visitation programs, try new things for God. It will be hard but you will try to walk on water. You will try to double your attendance. But some of you will be boat-sitters. You will argue that your youth group can't be doubled, just as those disciples argued that Peter couldn't walk on water. You boat-sitters need to try the impossible. Leave the safety of the boat. Walk on the water. When you begin to go down, the Lord will be there to save you, just as He saved Peter when he began to sink.

How many will jump to your feet as a testimony that you plan to double your youth group this year? You will say, "I can do all things through Christ which strengtheneth me—I can double my youth group."

THE DAY OF GREAT MEN
HAS NOT PASSED

Dr. Jerry Falwell preached this message over the radio March 15, 1972, as one of the regular Bible study messages of "The Old-Time Gospel Hour". During the spring of 1972 Falwell preached through the Book of Genesis. This message is included to show the content of radio messages by Falwell. Also, this sermon reflects a theme often emphasized by Falwell, that great men build great churches and that the day of great men has not passed. Some think the day of great men such as Luther, Wesley, and Moody has passed, that God is now emphasizing common men. The ministry of Jerry Falwell illustrates that God still raises up great men. Every preacher should read this message to stretch his vision and expectation.

11

THE DAY OF GREAT MEN
HAS NOT PASSED

Noah was an outstanding man. Today, God is looking for outstanding men. God is looking for outstanding preachers, pastors, Sunday-school teachers, bus captains, soul winners, missionaries, and evangelists. "Behold, I have given him for a witness to the people, a leader and commander to the people" (Isaiah 55:4). God's plan is that His flock is to be led by shepherds, not run by a board or a committee. God works through *men*. Committees are to advise, never to dictate. The Holy Spirit appoints *men* as bishops, pastors, and elders. God gives the care of the churches to these men, never to groups or committees. God's pastors are to be overseers—shepherds. Because churches have failed to recognize God's plan in working through *men*, there have been many, many heartaches and troubles. When God's plan is followed, all is well. The seven men designated in the Book of Acts as deacons had no voice in the management of the churches. They were chosen for the purpose of distributing daily food in an equal and orderly way. It was their business to serve the tables.

The Bible emphasizes *men*. If our nation is to be evangelized, it will be through godly men. Noah, Abraham, Isaac, Joshua, Moses --these were God's men. God has always worked through men. All Bible history gathers around men—their births, their lives, their work, their call, their successes and failures; the things they did, the things they taught and, finally, their deaths. Biographies hold a large place in the sacred record.

When God wanted a nation, he chose Abraham. In the days of famine in Egypt, Pharaoh had a one-man government. He chose Joseph, not a committee. When God wanted a deliverer, He called Moses. He might have gone to the elders of Israel and there selected a board, but He did not. His call came to one man. To him the Lord gave the vision, and Moses became God's representative, a great leader of his people. Moses died; now who was to carry on? Preachers die, pastors die, all of God's servants die. What happens to the work? What happened when Moses died? Did the people get together and choose a committee to guide them into the Promised Land? No! God sent another leader, an anointed man, for the task. His name was Joshua. Later, the Israelites got into difficulty. What did they do? Did they form a committee? No; they cried to God for a deliverer. They knew God's plan. They needed a leader, one man to whom they could look. God answered and sent Jehud, later Gideon, and finally Samson. And through all that dark period, God's plan operated. Judge after judge was sent until at last Samuel, the greatest of all judges and the first prophet, became their leader. As the years went by and another shepherd was needed, God told Samuel to anoint a little shepherd boy. The old leader, Samuel, died and left, not a committee, but a little shepherd boy; and David became the anointed shepherd of Israel, unified the nation, and conquered its enemies. Years later when the nation was backslidden, Elijah appeared. Each time the nation sinned, God raised up other great prophets, kings, and reformers to turn the people back to righteousness.

In the New Testament era, the pattern remained. First there was John the Baptist and then our precious Lord Jesus, God's only begotten Son. The local church was launched. How was it done—by a board? No, sir! By men filled with the Holy Ghost. Peter went to the Jews and Paul to the Gentiles. So the task was accomplished. Down through the ages we read of mighty reformers like Luther, Calvin, and Knox. Men were heralds of the reformation. Every time there is work to do and revival is needed, God looks for a man. Wesley was chosen—with him, Whitefield. Later Finney, Spurgeon, and Moody. When the foreign fields are to be reached, God touches the lives of men like William Carey, Adoniram Judson, David Livingstone, J. Hudson Taylor. They hear the call, they see the vision, they go.

What am I saying? We need some Noahs today. We need some men who will stand up and say, "I believe God. I believe what God says. I'll preach His Word. I'll stand upon the Bible." We have committees and organizations. They have their duties. Thank God for godly deacons and godly stewards and workers and leaders in local churches. But God never intended for a committee nor a board of deacons nor any other group to dominate a church or control a pastor. The pastor is God's man, God's servant, God's leader. When you tie the hands of God's man, when you keep him from acting as the Holy Spirit leads him, you have murdered his initiative, you have killed his spirit. All the great churches in our land are pastored by men, not committees. All the great congregations that are winning thousands to Christ, that I know anything about, have God's appointed man at the helm. God is looking for a Noah today that will get the ship built and get everybody inside before the judgment comes.

Spiritual stagnancy is a dangerous thing. For example, I have met Christians who at one time were on fire for the Lord but the fire went out. I was reading an article by Dr. Dale Oldham entitled, "Rote, Rut, Rot." The word *rote* is not very familiar to most us. It means "thoughtless routine," memorizing mere forms of speech without knowing the meaning. Christians practice rote by memorizing certain handed-down doctrines or by habitually repeating formerly significant phrases until the words have lost their freshness.

This is exactly what happens to God's people. Early in the life of Methodism, John Wesley was said to have expressed concern that Methodism might degenerate into a mere sect, losing its center, its aggressiveness, its zeal. Wesley recognized that any man's religion can go stale. One of the most deadly threats to any new religious movement is what William D. Carlson refers to as "second generationism." You may be a marvelous, dynamic Christian. You may have a walking, vital relationship with Christ, but your children must be taught to know Him personally as well. Christianity is something you cannot hand down. Christianity is something you cannot pass along, something you cannot give to others. Each new generation must accept it. Each person must receive Jesus Christ.

John Quincy Adams was a strict Puritan both in faith and morals. His son retained his father's morals but dropped his father's faith. His grandson dropped both faith and morals, so that in two short generations the total experince of the gospel was lost to that family.

If you and I are to preach convincingly, the Word of the Lord must maintain its freshness in our hearts. We must draw daily from the Bible's vigor, its inspiration, and its invitation to power. What a tragedy for the living gospel to degenerate to rote or routineness in any man's thinking, much less in the heart of a preacher or Sunday-school teacher or Christian worker. We need a new grip on God, a new understanding of fellowship, a new realization of what God wants to do through us. We must stand up and lead the way. We must say, "Follow me as I follow Christ." God wants to use you. God wants to use me. God is looking for a man who is available. That available man must be dependable. Are you willing to be both available and dependable to God today?

Noah found grace in the sight of the Lord. ". . . Noah was a just man and perfect in his generations, and Noah walked with God" (Genesis 6:9). That is why the Lord said to Noah, "Come thou and all thy house into the ark . . ." (7:1), and that is why, when the flood had subsided, "God remembered Noah . . ." (8:1). God remembered Noah and used Noah to repopulate the earth.

Now I want us to think about a man like Noah. We need men like Noah today. The Bible said he was a preacher of righteousness.

He preached for 120 years (6:3). Noah was a preacher. He was a powerful, dynamic preacher. He warned his neighbors by building an ark for the saving of his soul and the souls of his family. Noah followed God's blueprint. Noah was very careful to do everything God's way. Noah was a man of faith. It had never rained before. No water had ever come down from the sky. All the water had come as a mist up from the earth, yet God said water was going to come down from heaven. Noah believed that if God said it, it was so. Since God had said it, Noah believed it was going to rain. So Noah became God's choice vessel to save the world.

If you are a dedicated, Bible-believing, living-by-faith Christian you are going to be in the minority. If you are trying to be the most popular guy in town and are trying to win the "young man of the year" award, and if you are trying to make everybody like you— well forget it, God isn't going to use you very much. The Bible says, "Woe unto you, when all men shall speak well of you . . ." (Luke 6:26). I am sure Noah was the nut of his day. He was the religious fanatic of his hour. Can't you imagine what the thousands of people said when they saw that mammoth boat being built? Noah built a boat on dry ground, not by the waterfront. A boat so large—four hundred fifty feet long, seventy-five feet high and three tiers—can you imagine what the people were saying? Noah was preaching that as soon as he finished, the world would be destroyed. He preached that as soon as he laid down his hammer and nails, the world was going to be destroyed, covered by water. He preached repentance from sins. He preached that they had better get inside the ark. There was room for everyone. *Come,* was his message. The very fact that nobody came except his own family tells you what they were thinking.

". . .and the Lord shut him in" (Genesis 7:16). That means if you reject His offer of salvation, the day is coming when the door will be shut by God Himself and you won't have that second chance. When the door shut Noah in, it shut the world out. There was no hope and no help for those on the outside. Some of you listening to my voice right now—you are toying with death. You are toying with the fact that the Lord is coming soon. You are gambling with your soul. One day when God calls away His own, the Lord will have shut you out. One day when your heart stops beating you will have rejected Jesus Christ for your last time and the Lord will have shut you out. When God shuts the door, no man opens it.

We need some Noahs today—some men who will preach righteousness, some men who will preach judgment. I was speaking to the Congressional Prayer Breakfast in Washington last year and I told them that the destiny of our nation does not rest in their hands. It does not rest in the executive branch of the government or in the hands of the nine Supreme Court members. The desiny of our nation lies in the hands of the preachers and their willingness or unwillingness to preach the Word of God, to cry out against sin. I say to preachers everywhere, "You hold the destiny of America in your hands." A liberal preacher is not only an enemy of God, he's an enemy of the nation. For God has blessed this nation and honored America above all other nations. The Word of God has been preached here. Our forefathers were men who believed something —who were willing to pay a price and willing to die for the Bible and our land. We need men with backbone like Noah.

A recent magazine article carried a picture of the ancient Coliseum of Rome. Early Christians died there for a faith the world now takes for granted. Flavian Amphitheatre was and still is a showplace in Rome. It was built by Jewish slaves; the outside walls cost more than $50 million. It seated no less than fifty thousand people. Two thousand years ago gladiators and wild beasts fought there for public entertainment. One thousand animals were slain there on the Emperor's birthday. If we had sat in those grandstands amidst the grandeur that was Rome, we might have been deceived. The howling mob in the Coliseum did not determine the course of history. Underground in the catacombs, another force was working. A little handful of men and women who worshipped another King called Jesus—these changed history. Here was the beginning of an empire without an earthly emperor. The Christians crept along the subterranean passages, tunnels, and caverns among the tombs. They were hunted and persecuted. They were considered the scum of the earth. But if we had prowled around in those gloomy depths, we might have come upon little companies singing, listening to a gospel message, observing the Lord's Supper. We might have said, "They haven't a chance." But the underground Christians eventually upset the Caesars above ground. The catacombs overcame the Coliseum, and finally they put the amphitheatre out of business.

There's something fascinating about these saints of the catacombs. These citizens were on fire with a passion which swords could not kill, water drown, nor fire destroy. Their blood was spilled so freely in the arena that a traveler was asked once, "Do you want a relic? Take a handful of sand from the Coliseum—it is all martyrs."

But we are a pretty comfortable crowd of Christians. We know nothing of the spirit that motivated Noah. We know nothing of the spirit that motivated the saints of the catacombs. We have plenty of money, houses, cars, liberties, and everything that we call the American way of life. Yes, we're a comfortable crowd of Christians who seem to forget that the gospel is not a message to come to church to hear but the gospel is something to go from church to tell. The cause of Christ is not going to be carried forward by complacent Sunday-morning bench warmers who come in to sit but never go out to serve. Most of us have moved from the catacombs to the Coliseum. We are more interested in entertaining and being acknowledged than we are in winning men to Christ.

God remembered Noah because he was a just man, a perfect man in his generation. Noah walked with God. When God said, "Make thee an ark," Noah just started building. Everybody laughed, mocked, and said, "You're a religious nut." Some might have slurred, "You don't know what you're doing." Noah kept pounding away—building, sawing. One day the rain began to fall. The fountains of the deep were broken open and the windows of heaven were opened. Rain fell upon the earth forth days and forty nights.

If you want God to remember you, you've got to have a little spiritual backbone. You have got to be willing to be different. You have got to be willing to stand alone. You have got to be willing to be ridiculed, called names, misrepresented. You have got to be willing to pay the price. God is looking for giants who are not concerned about what the world thinks, but who are interested in pleasing the Lord. That was Noah.

WHAT MAKES A FAILURE?

Dr. Jerry Falwell preached this message at prayer meeting April 19, 1972, to approximately one thousand members. There were five visiting ministers in the congregation. Falwell wants every believer to have a successful Christian life. Those who are not successful, fail. The question remains, why do Christians fail in their attempts to live for God? This sermon attempts to answer that question. It is included to illustrate the type of message preached at prayer meetings.

12

WHAT MAKES A FAILURE?

Let's read Proverbs 16, verse 18. "Pride goeth before destruction, and an haughty spirit before a fall." There are many men and women in this building who have made a complete, miserable flop of their lives. Some of you here today realize that when you came to bat—you struck out. You have produced a zero. Your life has been non-plus. You can look back over your days and see very little excuse for your existence. Why do men fail? Why do lives fall apart? Why do homes crumble? What makes a failure?

History is replete with biographies of men who were total failures. I am selecting one failure from the Old Testament Book of Esther; his name was Haman. Haman was a failure. He was a total flop. His life was nonproductive. He damaged others and left a bad mark upon his society. Haman's contemporaries would have been better off if he had never been born.

In the Book of Esther, we have the story of God's provision for the Israelites during the time of captivity. The Jews had been dispersed among all the nations of the earth. The Persians ruled at that time. As the Medes and Persians dominated them, a handful of God's people had gone back to Palestine, but the majority were in spiritual lethargy.

The Book of Esther is unusual in that the name of God does not appear even one time. Yet there is no book in all the Bible that has more conspicuously shown the providential care of God for His own. The story of the Book of Esther is simply the story of the King of Persia, Ahasuerus, his wife, Queen Esther, and how God used

Esther and her Uncle Mordecai to preserve the Israelites from anni-
hilation. Since we're studying the life of a failure, we'll spend most
of our time not talking about Esther or Mordecai, but rather about
Haman.

"After these things . . ." (Esther 3:1). These three words refer
to the happenings of chapters 1 and 2. God in His providence had
Vashti removed as queen and elevated Esther, the sweet, godly girl,
to the place of queen. "After these things did King Ahasuerus
promote Haman the son of Hammedatha the Agagite, and advanced him, and set his seat above all the princes that were with
him." Haman was elevated to a high and prestigious place. Remember, "Pride goeth before destruction and an haughty spirit before a
fall." "Let him that thinketh he standeth take heed lest he fall" (1
Corinthians 10:12). The most dangerous place you will ever find
yourself is the place of exaltation—the place where you find yourself on top. Be careful when you are honored and revered by others. Somehow pride, that most dangerous foe of all, seems to creep
in during the hours of success and prosperity more than at any other time. Prosperity has always been the enemy of the cause of
Christ.

The churches were filled to overflowing back during the days of
the depression when men had little, when lives were destroyed financially, when economically things were going bad. During World
War II, the churches were bulging at the seams because millions of
our boys were out on battlefields facing hostile guns. Yet in times of
prosperity, like today, America finds itself going down the drain of
ecumenism, modernism, liberalism, immortality, indecency, and
permissiveness. Our nation is in trouble simply because we have
forgotten God. "Righteousness exalteth a nation: but sin is a reproach to any people" (Proverbs 14:34).

Haman was in a dangerous spot. He had been elevated. He had
been promoted to the second place in the kingdom. In that spot
pride began to take its toll.

I wonder how many Christians have followed the same trail. I wonder how many of you at one time had God's hand of blessing on you. God promoted you, elevated you, and used you greatly. But in spiritual stupidity you forgot the foundation of your strength, your life, and your ministry. I wonder how many of you have found that pride indeed "goeth before destruction and an haughty spirit before a fall." You are in a dangerous spot today if God is blessing you. Some here have been blessed financially. Some have lovely families, all in good health. You have money in the bank. You have a home in which to live. You have an automobile or two in which to travel. You have a good job. Your heart is beating. Blood is flowing through your veins. You breathe easily. You live in a rich and wealthy land, America. You have freedom. You have everything, humanly speaking, a man could desire, and yet you are ungrateful. You don't even bow your head over your plate and thank God for your meal. You don't even get your family together and sit down with an open Bible and pray. You don't say thank you for a Christian home.

Many of God's people have come from humble beginnings and have been blessed materially. Financially, God has multiplied you. But suddenly you have fallen in love with the almighty dollar. You have no time for God. You have no time for lost souls. You have no time for the things that are important. You have forgotten the rock from which you were hewn and the pit from which you were digged (Isaiah 51:1). Promotion and elevation are the beginning of a life that becomes a failure.

"And when Haman saw that Mordecai bowed not, nor did him reverence, then was Haman full of wrath" (Esther 3:5). Now, pride had its beginning. Haman was walking through the streets and everybody was bowing down to him, saying, "Oh, what a great man. Oh, what a prestigious person." But Haman walked by a Jew one day who would not bow down to him. His name was Mordecai, who had only one God. Like Daniel, Mordecai refused to bow down to the wrong person. He paid allegiance to one Master and one alone, his precious Lord. When Mordecai did not bow down to him, Haman became full of wrath.

I met a preacher not long ago who got very upset because a Christian friend did not refer to him as "doctor." He had a doctor's degree. He got that doctorate by working hard, but he met face-to-face with someone who still knew him as a brother. He said, "How are you doing, brother?" The preacher answered, "I'm 'Doctor' to you." Like Haman, no one was bowing down to him and he became angry.

God forgive us and deliver us from becoming position-conscious. Titles do not impress God and they should not impress you. We all put our shoes on the same way. We'll all stand before God one day. We'll all give an account. Whether you be a doctor, master, father, preacher, priest, or reverend, none of that will amount to the snap of the finger before Almighty God. Watch out for being easily offended because you're not elevated or recognized. Don't get your feelings hurt because you are left in the shadows of insignificance.

"And Haman told them of the glory of his riches, and the multitude of his children, and all the things wherein the king had promoted him, and how he had advanced him above the princes and servants of the king" (5:11). Now, elevation leads to jealousy, offense, pride, and boastfulness. Don't you hate to be around a braggart? Isn't it boring to be around somebody who overuses the personal pronoun *I?* Do you know somebody who can't talk without telling you about all of his accomplishments—where he's been, what he's done, who he knows? In the first place, bragging doesn't impress anyone. Boasting depresses me. Some preachers can't be around you five minutes without telling you who they are, where they've been and what they've done. Watch out! They're total flops and don't know it. If God is using you, if you're accomplishing something for the Lord, you don't have to talk about it. All you have to do is thank God, because every good gift and every perfect gift cometh down from God. "Naught have I gotten but what I have received." Paul said proud boasters are inventors of evil things (Romans 1:30). God deliver us from boastfulness!

We are talking about what makes a failure. We started off with *success*. We began moving along the trial of *pride*. Now we have come to *boastfulness*. "Then said Zeresh his wife and all his friends unto him, Let a gallows be made of fifty cubits high, and tomorrow speak thou unto the king that Mordecai may be hanged thereon: then go thou in merrily with the king unto the banquet. And the thing pleased Haman; and he caused the gallows to be made" (Esther 5:14). Now Haman was devising evil against his brethren. He was trying to hurt others. His pride and boastfulness produced maliciousness.

When hate gets into your heart, watch out. When bitterness takes its toll, watch out. A man who is bitter will become a failure. A man who has a grudge in his heart cannot succeed. A man who has a chip on his shoulder is on his way down. The reason many of God's servants cannot get the job done is that they are jealous and bitter toward someone else who is getting it done. God deliver us from professional jealousy.

Many of your homes are not what they ought to be, because husband and wife have bitterness toward each other. Bitterness is like cancer. If you allow it residence, it'll destroy you. Bitterness will literally eat you up. You show me a man who is filled with jealousy and bitterness and I'll show you a man who has created a miserable home for his wife and children. You show me a woman who is filled with wrath and has a malicious spirit and I'll show you somebody who has made a miserable home for her husband and children. Nothing destroys little children like being raised in hate. Little boys and girls break my heart when I go into homes where Mom and Dad raise the devil, drink liquor, fuss, feud, and fight.

Some parents think more of themselves than they do of their children. They are more interested in having their own way and hurting one another than they are in providing love, compassion, security, warmth, and kindness for those precious little children God has entrusted into their hands. The most important trust I have is the care of my three children. My wife and I will be held responsible before Almighty God for what we do with them.

"Yet all this availeth me nothing, so long as I see Mordecai the Jew sitting at the king's gate" (Esther 5:13). Haman said, "I can't enjoy my prominence so long as that Jew lives. So long as that fellow won't bow to me I can't enjoy life." Did you ever meet someone so full of hate he could not enjoy life? This hate-filled man passes a fellow employee in the factory or meets him in the aisle and it ruins his whole day. He's full of bitterness. So long as hate-cancer is in you, like Haman you are a failure, and your misery will be compounded.

"So Haman came in. And the king said unto him, What shall be done unto the man whom the king delighteth to honour? Now Haman thought in his heart, To whom would the king delight to do honour more than to myself" (6:6)? The king had heard Mordecai had saved his life away back and nothing had been done for him. The king wanted to honor Mordecai, so he asked Haman, "What shall I do for the man that I want to honor?" Well, Haman's chest stuck out and he said, "Sure that's me." And he felt nothing was too good for the man the king wants to honor. Haman told the king how to honor a man. The king said, "That is what I want to hear you say and so we will bring out the royal apparel. We will put the crown on this man. We will have the greatest banquet ever. We will honor the man that I delight to honor."

"Then the king said to Haman, Make haste, and take the apparel and the horse, as thou hast said, and do even so to Mordecai the Jew, that sitteth at the king's gate: let nothing fail of all that thou hast spoken" (verse 10). That must have broken his heart. Everything that he said ought to be done, let it be done to Mordecai the

Jew. Nothing could have hit Haman any harder between the eyes any worse than honoring the man that he hated.

The Scriptures give the very words that I think this man was facing in this hour. "To appoint unto them that mourn in Zion, to give unto them beauty for ashes, the oil of joy for mourning, the garment of praise for the spirit of heaviness; that they might be called trees of righteousness, the planting of the Lord, that he might be glorified" (Isaiah 61:3). Poor old Mordecai had been mourning. He had been going through heaviness, and God turned it all around, because the man who humbles himself will be exalted. The man who exalts himself will be humbled (Luke 14:11). Here, instead of the gallows for Mordecai it was the gallows for Haman.

"So they hanged Haman on the gallows that he had prepared for Mordecai. Then was the king's wrath pacified" (Esther 7:10). Later in Scripture we read, "He made a pit, and digged it, and is fallen into the ditch which he made" (Psalm 7:15). Haman failed because he became proud, self-centered, arrogant, malicious, jealous, and filled with bitterness toward another person. If you want to become a complete failure now that God has blessed you, forget where you came from. Become so self-centered that you're against everybody else that God blesses, and you're on your way down the drain.